What our readers are saying about...

Live from Strength!

"Live from Strength, by Wayne Ottum, is very direct and a pleasure to read. Short, to the point and organized in a way that has a natural flow. It affirms Wayne's gift of helping individuals truly realize what is most important to them, and shows them how to act now. This is not a book to just read once and put on the shelf... I plan to use it continually to create, plan, and adjust my life. This book will help me stay the course and live my dreams."
Diana Merritt, Mortgage Consultant

"Wayne Ottum keenly provides you with a process to hone in on the 'truth' within yourself that will allow you to create a life of value professionally and personally. His book deftly propels you to take action by identifying your strengths and encouraging you to create the answers that are right for you---accomplished in a manner that is not rigid or professorial. As a pragmatist and one who is not a devotee of the self-help book genre, the compelling, no-nonsense manner in which this book guides is invigorating and meaningful!"
Yvonne Salinas, Financial Planner

Live from Strength

*Discover your unique gifts and the incredible
power already within you!*

by

Wayne Ottum

with Deborah Kiernan-Ottum

Published by OE Press,
a Division of Ottum Enterprises, LLC

Copyright © 2014 Ottum Enterprises, LLC
218 Main St., #263
Kirkland, WA 98033
info@ottumenterprises.com
www.ottumenterprises.com

Cover design by Lauri Cook, iMarc Consulting, LLC
www.imarcconsulting.com

Library of Congress Control Number: 2013911328

ISBN-13: 978-0615836423

ISBN-10: 0615836429

Contents

Notes of Appreciation

There are many people to thank for helping me bring this book to you.

The biggest thank you and appreciation goes to my beautiful wife and business partner, Deborah Kiernan-Ottum. Literally, this book would never have become a reality without her. Not only is she the inspiration behind it being written, she took my raw concepts and thoughts and turned them into solid writing. She is also responsible for helping me improve the value of the process taught in this book, as through her counsel and feedback, the process was honed, sharpened, and expanded. Thus, this book and the process it teaches is a true product of both of us.

Together, we want to thank our family and friends for their continued support. To our children, Tessa, Jesse, Adrienne, Zac, and Mack, and our extended family, thank you for listening to our "crazy talk." Your love and belief in us and our vision warms our hearts. And thank you to our many friends who have encouraged us and put up with listening to our ideas (over and over again)!

A big thank you to Lauri Cook of iMarc Consulting, LLC. Lauri is a truly gifted marketing professional and creative designer and the talent behind our branding, marketing and book covers. She is an inspiration to us as we continue to watch her and her business grow.

A hearty thank you to our many clients who have inspired and encouraged us to share our ideas in this book and others. It is the success you have achieved that gives us the continued motivation to provide our services and find new and innovative ways to share our ideas.

Thanks to our many referral and business partners who provided valuable feedback, referrals and business contacts, and helped us grow our business.

Thank you to the many people we talked to who provided advice on the "how to's" of publishing, and willingly shared their time and expertise to help us get this book out to our readers.

We also wish to thank our book reviewers, Connie Tomlinson, Diana Merritt, Yvonne Salinas, Ruthann McVicker, and Marie Maguire, who willingly gave of their time to read the early drafts of this work. Your extraordinary and insightful comments were amazingly helpful. Without you, this book wouldn't be as good as it is now!

And thank you to you, our readers, for choosing this book from the many, many out there. It is our commitment to you to continue to challenge you to define and live, with purpose and intent, the life of your dreams. We trust you will find this book a valuable partner on your journey.

Introduction

This book is about one simple concept; how to *Live from Strength...* It is about claiming and experiencing positive, affirming, personal power. The POWER to *live* the life of your dreams, TODAY! It is the POWER that comes from defining a "clarity of direction" that naturally compels you forward to achieve the success you desire. It is the POWER and fulfillment that you feel when you discover and embrace your unique purpose, your reason for being. It is the POWER that comes from a clear sense of self and the feeling of authenticity and personal integrity that comes from living true to the real you. It is the POWER of a simple, no nonsense and proven process that challenges you to discover your unique gifts and define the life you desire while challenging you to live it, with purpose, intent, and authenticity, each and every day. It is the POWER of a simple process that not only feels genuine to you as you go through it, but yields results that are unique and authentic to you!

This book is also about living and acting with confidence. It is about confidently choosing to live, **on purpose**, in alignment with your unique gifts. It is about living with integrity, in alignment with your authentic self, filled with confident, purposeful and intentional action that drives you toward the very success you envision for yourself. It is about living a lifestyle that is positive and affirming; one that allows you to let go of the past and those things that hold you back and instead directs your focus on your strengths and unique and natural abilities so you can live today with confidence. This book is about making the most of the only period of time each of us is ever given – TODAY, this moment! It is about making each and every day an opportunity to live your best life. It is about a focus on the present and taking confident action TODAY, and every day, to do the things that are most likely going to lead you to the success you desire.

There is also an element of personal *challenge*. The challenge to discover your unique gifts and how to use them to their fullest to create real and meaningful value for yourself and for those you serve, finding true meaning in your existence. It is facing the challenge to learn and discover real personal POWER by clearly defining the life you desire and finding the courage to purposefully, intentionally and confidently choose that life TODAY, and every day, with each and every decision you make. And it is standing up to the challenge to live and act each day with integrity, by being true to the real you; and to forgive yourself, so you can get back on track quickly when things don't quite go as planned.

Extraordinary *personal fulfillment* is the result of living from strength. You know who you are and where you are going. You are in control of your life, your destiny. You know why you are here; you understand your gifts and how they bring meaning to your life and to your world. You are confident and self-assured. Challenges are opportunities and decisions are now easy for you to make. You are happy, living an authentic life; a life that resonates with you. This is true fulfillment. In fact, we are confident that when you discover the real you and begin to practice living intentionally, on purpose, and with authenticity, you will discover and experience all these things for yourself. There is no greater feeling of fulfillment.

This is how you *Live from Strength*! This is the power of the process we teach you in this book. But more than just a process, this book explores a way of life you may not have thought about before, a lifestyle based on your true and natural gifts. And it explores a new way of thinking of yourself, one where you LIVE the life of your dreams, each and every day. This book guides you to discover your own unique gifts and the true POWER this brings you as an individual. It provides a no-nonsense, practical method for creating a personal plan for your life that is truly unique, and in alignment with you. As importantly, you learn to BELIEVE in yourself and in your own power so you can act confidently and successfully, each and every day.

Imagine Living from Strength

Imagine what it means to *Live from Strength!* Imagine knowing and understanding your unique gifts and the value these gifts bring to your world. We encourage you to read each paragraph below and then close your eyes and allow yourself to feel the power and confidence that comes from knowing and believing!

Imagine knowing, with clarity and calm resolve, what you really desire. Imagine knowing your **direction**, where you are going in your life and why. Imagine being drawn, compelled even, to take action each day to create and live this exciting life that you envision!

Imagine knowing, and feeling empowered by, where you are TODAY, in this moment, in relationship to the direction you have defined for your life. Imagine the invigorating feeling of confidence waking each day knowing what you need to do TODAY to move you in the direction you want to go.

Imagine knowing the unique and incredible gifts (strengths, talents, and abilities) you bring to this world and, more importantly, knowing that they ARE unique, powerful and valuable. And imagine the empowering feeling of knowing how to use your gifts most effectively to create **purpose** and meaning in your life.

Imagine the feeling of gratitude and peace of mind knowing you are fairly and abundantly compensated, financially and emotionally, for the value these unique gifts provide to those you serve. Imagine financial abundance!

Imagine using your gifts to create a clear **purpose** in life and discovering the answer to the question, *"Why am I here?"* Imagine having a clear purpose and a solid sense of personal fulfillment. Imagine this knowledge confidently guiding your day-to-day actions in your chosen profession and your personal life. Now imagine the affect this knowledge would have on creating a positive, affirming sense of self.

Imagine a life focused on all that is good in you, discovering, enhancing and developing your strengths to encourage and enhance the value you provide. Imagine truly, honestly and completely believing in yourself, having ultimate confidence in who you are, where you are, and what you do.

Imagine being at a crossroads in your life and needing to make a tough decision before you can move forward. How do you feel? Conflicted? Confused? Scared? Now imagine making these decisions with clarity, consistency and confidence every time, knowing your decisions are in alignment with who you are. Imagine decisions being made simply and easily. Imagine living with this kind of personal **integrity**!

Imagine knowing your daily plan of action and having that feeling of confidence and certainty that the effort you are making TODAY is leading you to the very success you desire.

Imagine knowing where your center is, where you are. Imagine having a set of tools you can use over and over again to help you get back to center, to find your way home during those times when life happens and causes a hiccup or two. Tools, at the ready, that keep you on course, and continually guide your life's journey as you change and grow, as the world changes around you, and as you reach and achieve your desires. Imagine knowing yourself so well that you can always find your way back to center.

This is what it means to *Live from Strength*! This is the power of the process we teach you in this book. It is not a one-size-fits-all approach. This unique process provides a no-nonsense, practical method for creating a plan for YOUR life that is truly personal, truly unique, and truly in alignment with you. We challenge you to explore a new way of life and a new way of thinking of yourself that opens doors for you to do more than simply imagine a life well lived. It challenges you daily to *Live from Strength*!

Who Lives Such a Life?

It is one thing to imagine being different and living the life of your dreams, but who actually *lives* a life of direction, purpose and integrity? Who lives a life of POWER, confidently LIVING each and every day the life they desire, built on a solid foundation of their unique gifts. To answer this question, let's share a few powerful results from our clients (though the names may not be real, the stories are)...

Kathy was a twenty-something former Olympian. Her parents, having sacrificed much to support the goals of an Olympic athlete, believed that their daughter would have an "Olympic-sized life and career." So, naturally, they prepared her for and pushed her in that direction and Kathy set out to create just that. But along the way, she began to question "Why?" and worked with us to define the life she truly desired. To the surprise of everyone around her, she was able to clarify something she had always known; she desired a simpler lifestyle of being a loving wife and a good mother, a domestic engineer, far from the pressure of Olympic-sized expectations. She discovered that what she was doing daily was in direct conflict with what she really desired for herself. Armed with her clear vision of her authentic life, Kathy turned away from her high powered career and turned toward what she truly desired. I remember fondly the delight she expressed in the cards she sent announcing the arrival of her first, and then second, child! She had discovered *her* unique purpose and was blissfully living a life of true alignment!

Ben was in sales and starting a family with his wife. He needed greater focus and direction in his life to better support his family, but did not know how to create it. While working with us, he discovered that his passion, his unique purpose, was coaching. But he knew coaching Little League would not pay the bills. Through further exploration, however, Ben discovered there were many professions where "coaching" was the unique skill needed to be successful and he eventually moved into and excelled in his new career as a "financial coach" while more than adequately supporting his new family!

Lauri is a marketing professional who, because of her family, thought she needed the security of a "full-time job." But she longed to do more within her profession. She had a dream to create her own marketing company, but she did not have a plan and didn't understand her unique gifts. After working with us, she discovered her true strengths and "fired" her employer because she had developed the confidence that comes from aligning herself to her unique gifts and trusting in her own ability. She started her own firm and continues to successfully live her dream TODAY!

Rob owned a plumbing company. But more than anything else, the plumbing company owned Rob while he labored to manage the day-to-day operations of the business. He came to us to help him plan for success in his company, but discovered in the process what he knew intuitively; that he was NOT cut out for a life in the plumbing business. He discovered his unique gifts were not to *operate* a business, but rather to buy, improve and sell businesses! So his plans changed and so did Rob. He was no longer ruled by the business. He created his own rules and built a plan to rejuvenate and sell his plumbing business as the first in a series of many such turnaround successes!

Debra was a wife and mother and believed she needed a steady job to help support her family. But she longed to do something more significant in her life. Working with us she rediscovered what she had longed to do since she was a teenager. Her true desire was to own a dress shop, but not just any dress shop, a shop that provided a warm, uplifting and supportive environment for all women. Within weeks of completing our process, she was acting on her plan, working in retail establishments to build the experience and confidence needed to step out on her own. Debra began living the life of her dreams, not just waiting for it to happen.

Cindy is smart, ambitious, talented and young. She was also in a very controlling and abusive relationship. Within weeks of working with us she found the confidence in herself to leave that relationship and take control of her real estate and acting career. It was not long before she moved to Los Angeles and the bright lights!

Julia is an attorney. But Julia was also, self proclaimed, a little "quirky." You see, she and her father (and her other siblings) have a unique sense of humor, and a different way of looking at life. Nothing wrong with that unless you believe, like Julia did, that being a lawyer requires you to act a certain way, perhaps a little more "normal." After working with us, however, Julia realized that her unique personality and way of thinking was also her unique gift, allowing her to provide her clients with "out of the box" solutions to their varying legal issues. In short, what she once thought of as a weakness was actually her greatest strength; and when understood and used positively, it became her unique purpose.

Mark worked in the crowded financial services market. He "thought" he had found his calling but was not seeing the success he believed he should be seeing; and, more importantly, he wasn't having as much fun as he thought he should be having if this was his "true calling." After working with us, Mark discovered that he was right aligned with his career choice, but that success and fulfillment were not coming to him because he was not applying his unique gifts to his practice. Instead of following the "proven model" for success in the financial services industry, Mark discovered that he had to chart his own course, one better aligned with his strengths. When he stopped fighting himself and incorporated his natural way of learning, communicating, and motivation style, his success came quickly and so did the fun and his sense of personal fulfillment!

So, to answer the question, *"Who lives such a life?"* A life of direction, purpose and integrity; a life of fun, fulfillment, and success; a life of personal alignment; a life focused on one's strengths? *The answer is people just like you!* People who accepted the challenge to define for themselves a clear direction, who now know and use their unique gifts daily to create value in the world, and who follow a chosen path defined by their own values! People who simply have chosen to act, with purpose and intent, to live the life of their dreams, each and every day. People like you who have discovered how to *Live from Strength*!

Why Doesn't Everyone Live This Way?

WOW, what a question! When the concept of living a life of direction, purpose, and integrity is simple, non complex and straightforward, why doesn't everyone live this way? To answer this question, let's begin to explore it from another point of view, from your experience. First, answer the following questions: From your perspective, how many people in our society live a successful life? What percentage are empowered and fulfilled and living the life of their dreams every day? Ten percent? Five percent? Maybe less? Think about your friends, family, and co-workers. How many of them are living a life of direction, purpose, and integrity, energized and fulfilled?

When we ask these questions in our seminars, the general consensus is always less than 10% and usually closer to one percent! Whatever your answer is, we can readily agree that only a small percentage of people are actually living the life of their dreams.

So, *why?* Why do so few live the life they truly desire? Why do people remain in dead-end jobs, bad relationships, or fail to take risks to go after what they really want in their life? Is it simply a lack of information? No. A recent search on a popular internet bookseller site for the phrase *"personal growth,"* revealed over 50,000 results! So it is clear to us that there is a lot of information available to help people learn how to live a truly successful life.

Is it an issue of inadequate information and resources? We don't think so. Many authors, from Napoleon Hill, to Steven Covey, to Wayne Dyer, to Louise Hay, and the wonderful principles they teach have helped millions of people make positive changes so they could live better lives.

Perhaps the issue, then, is whether the information is being presented in a way that makes sense to most people? Could it be that these noted authors provide great information, but that this information is only a piece of the overall puzzle for most people? Is there some missing fundamental concept that would help people better utilize this valuable information?

Or could it be that perhaps living a life of purpose, intent, and authenticity is simple in concept, but too challenging in reality, so too few boldly strike out to live it? Could it be that our dreams and desires seem so large and too far away that we can't figure out what the first step is, or what "one thing" we need to do today to get us where we want to go?

In our work, we found the answers to be a bit of "all of the above." *Live from Strength* is the result of a lifetime of work, nearly 30 years, as students and practitioners of business and personal development. It is a result of our continually asking the question, *"Why?"* Why do so few live a truly purposeful life? Why, with all this information, do so many still seek answers? Why does it seem so hard for most people to define and live the life of their dreams? Why were our clients seeking us out to help them achieve success when many of them had already read the great authors, had taken many personal growth courses, were highly educated, and had even tried a few non-traditional methods? Why were people still not acting intentionally, purposefully and authentically, each day? And why, in our early years when we started our practice and with our lifetime of accumulated knowledge, were we not able to make more of a positive difference for our clients? All of these "whys" and more really got us thinking...

So then we began to ask, "How?" *How* do we take all this great information and all these wonderful success principles and put them into effective practice for our clients? Trial and error was not working, and, quite frankly, consumed too much time and energy. Some of the principles could be adopted quickly and created great results for some, but limited results for others, while other principles just didn't seem to stick at all for our clients. With all this information available and with thousands of people and business owners trying them on for size and still not finding the full success they desired, we concluded there must be something fundamentally missing.

And so began our search for concrete, no-nonsense answers to these perplexing questions. Answers that would ring true to most people and create real value by helping them live the life they truly desire. We searched for tools that were practical, usable and created real results. We looked for a process that allowed each individual to create a customized result that embodied their unique talents, needs, and beliefs. In our search, we came to realize three things were needed:

- **Clarity** - of direction, purpose and authenticity.

- **Simplicity** - of the process for defining and maintaining clarity.

- **Challenge** - in life for meaning and fulfillment.

We Need Clarity

Though there is a great amount of information available to the masses, we discovered, as individuals, we also need a **clearly defined foundation**, or filter, to allow us to effectively make sense of the vast information available. We discovered that this foundation, this filter, consisted of the following fundamental components: clarity of direction, a defined purpose, and a set of personal values. That is, it means defining your own *authentic self*. An authentic self where your purpose, or mission in life, is based on the unique gifts you bring the world. It is a compelling vision stating where you are going in your life and career that defines true success, and intentionally focuses your day-to-day activities on creating and living that vision. It is a meaningful set of values (or ethics) that guide your decision making. All combined, your unique vision, purpose, and values, you now have the framework (the foundation) in which to evaluate this vast array of information.

Knowing your *authentic self* and the definition of *true success* as you define it for your life gives you the filter to quickly evaluate the many options and possibilities presented, quickly glean those ideas that are in alignment with who you are, and create a *meaningful* plan for success that truly resonates with you individually. Without this filter, *everything* seems a possibility and any answer that worked for others might also work for you. The result is chaos, endlessly trying new ideas, most likely feeling like a pinball bouncing from bumper to bumper but not finding what you seek, a clear direction or purpose.

As we worked with our clients to help them define this filter for themselves, they found that clarity lead to ease! That is, in general, life became easier and their "dis-ease" seemed to melt away. It became easier for them to make decisions. It became easier to focus on what really mattered to them and let the things that didn't (time wasters) fall away. It became easier to adopt or adapt the great ideas and teachings they read in books or heard in seminars in a way that worked best for them. And for the first time, it became easier to act, each day, with purpose, intent, and authenticity because their purpose, intent, and authenticity had been clearly defined in a way that made total sense to them!

A Simple Process of Self Discovery

To achieve clarity in life we realized **a process of personal self-discovery was required**. This process had to be simple and resonate with most people so it could be reasonably managed and accomplished. It also had to produce results that were practical, effective, and felt genuine. And so began our search. To our surprise, however, we did not find a tried-and-true process already developed and outlined, or at least none that resonated with *most* people. There are, however, many methodologies and practices of personal self-discovery available, but we found none that were simple, comprehensive and complete that could truly adapt to the unique talents, needs, and beliefs of most people, allowing them to create personalized and meaningful results.

It became clear to us that there was a great need for a simple, practical and no-nonsense process to help people build their personal foundation so they could make sense of all this great information *in a way that resonated with their unique needs*, and we realized we would have to create this simple process ourselves.

It Is Still a Challenge

Of significant importance, we discovered that **building the life of your dreams and living a life of true alignment based on these fundamentals is a *challenge*.** That is, it is a challenge to truly assess yourself, to look deep within and decide once and for all *who you are* and *what you want*. Though the *concept* of living a life intentionally, purposefully, and with integrity may be simple, actually defining and living this life can be a challenge. Or said another way, we discovered that many believe the status quo (going with the flow, letting life happen to you, or being the pinball in someone else's life) is far easier and less risky than taking control of the "flippers;" accepting the challenge to define and hold yourself accountable to a life of direction, purpose and integrity. Further, some may believe such a life is a pipe dream or perhaps they had tried before, many times, and failed so the challenge to try again now feels too overwhelming.

With additional research and testing, however, we discovered this very challenge is actually what was needed to *motivate* most people to act and live their best life. We knew from our own life and career, from those we studied, and from those we guided, that living life *on-purpose* is one of the most wonderful and rewarding challenges we can experience! In fact, studies have shown that people need to be challenged to achieve great things. A 2009 study by Princeton University President Emeritus William Bowen, lead author of *Crossing the Finish Line: Completing College at America's Public Universities*, found that graduation rates actually INCREASED as a function of the difficulty of the coursework. This theory is further exemplified by a quote from Ronald E. Osborn, noted religious author, scholar, and teacher, *"Undertake something that is difficult; it will do you good. Unless you try to do something beyond what you have already mastered, you will never grow."* Well said, indeed!

We realized, therefore, that *challenge* was a multi-faceted, integral, and necessary part of life in order to *Live from Strength!* Not only is it a challenge to define and live a life of purpose, direction, and integrity, it is perhaps THE most rewarding and glorious challenge you will ever face. Not only is it a challenge to act each day with purpose and intent, but we discovered that we, in our practice, needed to focus on challenging our clients to do just that because, in the end, it was exactly what they needed to reach their full potential.

The Result

As we clearly identified the components needed, we began our quest to create a simple, practical, no-nonsense and effective process of personal self-discovery and individualized planning. We desired to create a process that would work and make sense for most people, allowing them to discover their unique gifts and live a life based on their STRENGTHS; a process that would allow them to apply their own personal beliefs to the process and their results. Results, compelling and personally meaningful to them, that would lead to a simple and actionable plan to achieve their personal dreams. A process and methodology to help them dream about and then LIVE, each and every day, the life they truly desire. A highly personalized process that guided them through the challenge of creating clarity in their life that continued to challenge them to achieve success as they defined it!

The end result was the *Personal Growth Challenge*™ - a one-on-one coaching program to help individuals clearly define the life of their dreams and build the plan to achieve it. Using all the knowledge, skills, and experience of a lifetime, we began developing this trademarked process, taking our clients through each component, and improving and adding to it based on feedback and results.

Here is what one of our *Personal Growth Challenge*™ clients said about this life changing process:

"Your process and coaching methodology helped me to clearly define my own values, create a unique and compelling vision for my life, align my career to my strengths and passions, and to define meaningful goals and objectives for my life. What was great was that I was not forced into some boilerplate plan. Instead, your process challenged me to create a plan that uniquely represents my own vision, values, and goals. The result has left me energized and confident that I am on the right track; and, for the first time, I am excited about my future."
Ben B., Kirkland, Washington

And you can do it too! Are you ready to accept the challenge to define and live the life of your dreams? Are you ready to *Live from Strength*? If you are, then give your authentic self a voice, and give this book a chance! Jump into each exercise with both feet and explore yourself to the fullest. Use the methods in this book to develop your personal foundation, based on your unique gifts, and commit to the process for one year. We are extremely confident you will find success, as you define it, and you will be well on the road to the life you desire with the tools needed to get there. And most important, rather than waiting around for your dreams to come true, you will feel, perhaps for the first time that you are actually LIVING the life of your dreams!

If you're excited to get started after reading this introduction, feel free to jump ahead to Section I to begin your journey through this exciting process of self-discovery.

If, however, you need more background and a better overview of the process and outcomes you will create during this process, please continue reading in the next section.

Living from Strength

"Always bear in mind that your own resolution to success is more important than any other one thing."
Abraham Lincoln

Understanding the power and confidence that is yours when you *Live from Strength* begins with understanding what makes a successful life.

Through a review of much of the acclaimed literature written over the last 100+ years regarding success, whether personal, team or business, we discovered and believe the basic principles of personal success boil down to three things:

- A clearly defined strategy to achieve success in your life, as YOU define it…

- An honest and complete assessment of the current state of your ability to deliver on the strategy to achieve personal success…

- Intentional, purposeful, authentic and focused daily action to achieve your vision…

In 1928, Napoleon Hill and Dale Carnegie wrote a training course entitled, *The Law of Success*, which became Hill's classic, *Think and Grow Rich*. Carnegie went on to write, *How to Win Friends and Influence People,* and built a teaching empire on the concepts of personal development. Earl Nightingale, considered by many the Dean of the modern personal development movement, authored and spoke the classic audio cassette series, *Lead the Field*. More recently, Steven Covey wrote, *The Seven Habits of Highly Effective People*. All of these great, timeless classics, when boiled down to their essence, teach us that success in life is about creating a clear strategy, completing an honest and detailed assessment of one's ability to deliver on that strategy, and intentional, purposeful, principled, and focused daily action on that strategy.

In the area of a clearly defined strategy, this literature continually refers to three basic strategic principles:

- **A Compelling Vision** – A compelling vision is "a view of your life" at some point in the future, given what is known today. It embodies what you want from life, and it provides the compelling emotional reasons for why these things are desired. In short, this is *success*, as you define it. It is the emotional driver for being and becoming all you truly desire.

- **A Clear Purpose, or Mission, in Life** – A clear and properly defined purpose, or mission, is your reason for being. It is the unique value that you provide the world and it is how you create meaning in your life.

Such a clear purpose leads directly from your unique gifts and abilities and when discovered and honed, can provide something of value that others will "purchase," either in terms of ideas, work, or even works of art. It is here that so many people are most stymied in their journey through life; by not believing in, discovering, or understanding that they DO, without a doubt, have unique and valuable gifts. Everyone does! And it is this fact that is the underlying premise of *Live from Strength!*

- **A Set of Core Values** – Values are the unbreakable rules by which you lead your life. The ethics you hold dear and will not willingly violate. They are the moral compass that guides decision making so that when tough decisions need to be made you can quickly determine which decisions are in alignment with your core values, and discard those that are not.

A Foundation for Personal Success

These components, **vision** (direction), **mission** (purpose), and **values** (ethics), are foundational to a successful personal strategy for life for a number of reasons:

- **They define success.** Success is achieving the vision and fulfilling the mission by delivering the promised value while making a living and while (most likely) helping others achieve their dreams (feed their families, continue their education, etc.).

- **They focus action.** The personal mission focuses the daily activities of life on continually building and improving your unique gifts to create ever greater value and delivering on the promised value of these gifts whether to employers, clients or loved ones, depending on your chosen purpose.

- **They define measurement.** Since success is defined, progress toward it can be measured. Meaningful goals can be set, managed against, and achieved.

- **They guide and align decision making.** Core values determine when choices have to be made and which choices will move you toward your defined vision (success).

- **They determine how to evaluate performance.** Simply put; you are performing optimally when you are doing those things each day that drive you toward your stated vision and deliver on your defined mission, all while acting with integrity. What else is there?

- **They create an emotional drive for success.** When the story of success is compelling and your reason for being is clear, you can confidently act each day knowing you are doing what is truly right for you.

- **They create the ideal conditions for fulfillment and fun.** When your life is aligned and you are living with purpose and authenticity, life is simply much more enjoyable. As important, you can experience guilt-free fun knowing that the most important thing you "should" be doing in this moment, is recreating and having fun.

Thus, you have the best chance of achieving success and personal fulfillment by implementing a clear and compelling vision that you believe in, focusing daily action on developing and delivering your unique gifts, delivering on your unique value, and making decisions that are aligned to your core values. By doing so, you feel valued because your focused efforts create real results and real value to others, AND you feel greater fulfillment and alignment in your life while having a hell of a lot more fun!

In short, creating this personal strategic foundation for yourself (by defining your vision, mission, and values) and living a life where you intentionally act to create your vision, purposefully using your unique gifts to provide value, while making decisions with integrity, increases the very likelihood of success and feelings of fulfillment and enjoyment in that success.

What IS a "Life Well Lived?"

Steven Covey, in his extraordinary book, *The Seven Habits of Highly Effective People*, provides a very valuable visual exercise we like to use in our practice to help people focus on what is most important to them...

Take a moment now to imagine yourself at YOUR funeral. As you are being eulogized, what is everyone saying about you and the life you lived? What would you want them to say that would make your life sound like a "life well lived?" Really take a few minutes to think about this. How would you like to be remembered? Now write your own eulogy.

You will likely find several principles in your newly written eulogy that we believe embody most of what one might desire in a "life well lived." We've listed many of them here:

- **Purpose** – Living a life of purpose means you are engaged in work you believe provides value, where you clearly understand that value and feel connected to - and passionate about - your contribution. This is a place where you are valued and appropriately compensated, both financially and emotionally, for that value. This is having a life of meaning.

- **Direction** – Living a life of direction means you are absolutely clear on where you are going in your life, knowing the difference between your needs and wants, and what is truly important to you. This is a life where you confidently act each day to move in that defined direction.

- **Integrity** – Living a life of integrity means living according to a *defined* set of unwavering values that guide your decision making along your journey and keeps you true to yourself. This is the real meaning of integrity – being honest with yourself and being true to you.

- **Alignment** – Living a life of alignment means first understanding your unique talents and strengths and then aligning your vocation and avocations to your unique gifts and to your life's purpose. It means knowing who you are, and just as importantly - *who*

In-teg-ri-ty: noun: adherence to moral and ethical principles; soundness of moral character; honesty.

you are not* - which includes *knowing* what your unique strengths are and how to use them to create and sustain your individual purpose and direction.

- **Focus** – Living a life of focus means *intentionally* (on purpose) focusing your energy and activities on those things that utilize your strengths, activates on your purpose, leads you toward your chosen direction, and keeps you aligned to your true self. This also means choosing *not* to act outside your true self on time wasters and destructive activities and habits.

- **Balance** – Living in balance means finding and staying centered to your core beliefs, your true self. It can also mean having an effective work-life balance, or as we prefer to think about it, an effective *"work-life integration,"* where one's work supports one's life and vice-versa, and where neither is "competing" for your time and attention. Or balance may simply mean having a feeling of being centered, in tune with nature or your religious beliefs, etc. *Balance* can be defined as however you might describe the peaceful feeling of alignment and calm in your life.

- **Mastery** - As Daniel Pink discusses in his book *Drive,* all people desire to become a master, a true expert, at something. Thus, living a life of mastery means discovering your unique gifts and intentionally, purposefully and continually developing them into true strengths. Strengths that will allow you to become a master in whatever field is in alignment with your unique gifts.

- **Enjoyment** – Living a life of enjoyment is not only about having fun along the way, but having a positive attitude about life during the journey. It is living a life of gratitude and appreciation for all that you have and acknowledging the gift of opportunity – the opportunity to challenge yourself to live your dreams.

This is certainly not a complete list of statements used to define a life well lived, but given these descriptions, let's try a little experiment:

Read the following list of statements. As you do, be aware of your feelings and how you react to these statements deep down. Ask yourself how defining your life in these terms makes you feel:

- I work in a dead end job that sucks the life out of me.

- I dread each Sunday night knowing that I have to get up the next morning to face yet another week of agonizing monotony.

- I feel I am just going through the motions, reacting to life as it happens TO me and as others tell me what to do.

- My life, my relationships, and my career suck.

- I have to work way too hard to get anywhere in life.

- I never have enough money.

- The world and all the people in it are against me.

How are you feeling?

NOW, read the following list of statements. Once again, be aware of your feelings and reactions and ask yourself if you feel different, more positive, or more alive:

- I know where I am going in my life and feel good about my direction.

- I provide real value to those I serve and I am fairly and adequately compensated for my work.

- I love what I do and I can't wait to get started each day.

- My life has real purpose and meaning.

- I am focused, doing the things I need to do to get where I want to go in life.

- My career is on the right track, fulfilling and rewarding.

- My relationships are warm, positive and healthy.

- I truly appreciate all the love and respect I receive from those around me.

- I feel in alignment. I am honest with myself and I know I am being true to the real me.

- I am excited about each new day and the possibilities it brings.

- I have an abundance of financial resources and the money I need comes to me easily.

Give yourself a few moments to ponder the difference in how these lists of statements made you feel when you read them. Dig deep and be honest with yourself.

Perhaps you are doing OK. You are getting along and paying the bills. You have a nice family and good friends, but you just seem to be missing that spark in life. Perhaps you have an itchy feeling, thinking there must be more to life but just don't know how to get there.

The truth is - everyone *desires* to live a life of direction, purpose and integrity. We would not intentionally live a life void of these important life aspects. In addition, we would not intentionally define our life using the negative statements in the first list. We do, however, often fall into these counter-productive thought patterns when we don't have the positive definition of a life of direction, purpose and integrity for our life to replace them and more effectively guide us in a way that feels right for us.

The problem is most of us don't know *how* to create such a life, let alone live it. Most of us did not learn these skills from our parents, or in school, nor were we given the tools to create and sustain this mind set, this lifestyle, throughout our lifetime. Many of us may not know the true value of living this way because we have never experienced it ourselves, or witnessed it in our parents or others in our lives. So we don't know how rewarding, fulfilling and fun it can be! In short, we may not know what we don't know... and we may not know what we are missing.

In an attempt to replace these negative ideas, many have embarked on a journey of self discovery by trying various types of "self-help" programs such as visioning, defining values, goal setting, list making, and other "keys to success." All are very valuable pieces of life's puzzle. *The Personal Growth Challenge*™ **process provides the** *connection* between these puzzle pieces in one cohesive, comprehensive, understandable program of continual self-development that rings true to who YOU are. Let's state that again because it bears repeating... Finding a personal success program that resonates and aligns with the real you, one that allows your authentic self to shine through, is what it's all about! We are talking about a fully-customized strategy, assessment tool and plan that makes all of the connections specifically for, and personalized to YOU!

As discussed earlier, the connection that ties it all together to provide the definition of a life well lived, are the same three foundational and fundamental components found in all the great books about personal success:

- A clear and compelling **vision** of the life desired. This defines your success and creates a meaningful direction.

- A defined purpose or **mission** in life. A purpose gives your life meaning, creates the conditions for alignment and personal fulfillment, and focuses daily actions.

- A set of unwavering **values** to guide daily decision making. Values define your balance or center, and allow true happiness and fulfillment, knowing you are living in alignment with who you are.

So you see, to *Live from Strength* truly is a powerful, affirming and effective way to live! It's the connection that ties it all together. It provides a true and real foundation for your life; a clearly articulated *personal strategy* that consists of your vision of a life well lived, your unique purpose (mission), and embodies your unique talents, and a set of core values that guide your decisions. To *Live from Strength* also must include an honest and detailed *assessment* of where you are today regarding your alignment to, and ability to deliver on, that strategy. And finally, you must have a *"plan of action"* that focuses your daily activities on achieving and fulfilling your dreams.

When packaged and presented in this way, your clearly articulated strategy becomes your *Personal Strategic Foundation.* Assessing where you are now and your ability to deliver on your strategy becomes your *Current State Assessment.* And your focused plan of action becomes your *Personal Annual Action Plan.*

Thus, the *Personal Growth Challenge*™ provides the process and tools for creating the incredible power, confidence and personal fulfillment that comes when you *Live from Strength.* If you are excited and can't wait to get started, feel free to go directly to page 55 to begin and prepare for your *Personal Growth Challenge*™.

If, on the other hand, you desire a more thorough examination of the *Personal Growth Challenge*™ process, then the next sections are for you. We will review each of these components more closely before we break them down into step-by-step exercises.

The *Personal Growth Challenge*™ Process

The *Personal Growth Challenge*™ process consists of five simple components, or steps, as defined in the following diagram:

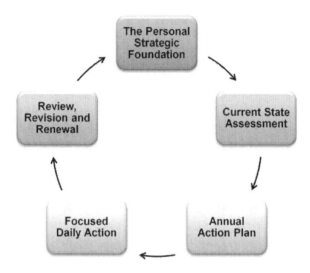

Figure 1: The *Personal Growth Challenge*™ Process

- **Creating your Personal Strategic Foundation** defines your authentic self and the life you truly desire through your written direction (vision), purpose (mission), and guiding principles (values).

- **Completing a Current State Assessment** determines where you are today in relation to the life you truly desire, as outlined in your Personal Strategic Foundation, and helps you prioritize what is most important to you, listing what needs your attention right now.

- **An Annual Action Plan** guides you to create clear and meaningful goals based on your current assessment.

- **Focused daily action**. It all happens today, in this moment, and today is really all we have control over. Taking intentional, purposeful, focused, daily action and doing so with confidence, knowing these are the actions most likely in alignment with the vision you defined as being the life of your dreams.

- **Completing periodic and annual reviews, revisions, and renewals.** Things change, you change, you reach your objectives and, sometimes, you may stray off course. This process provides tools for periodic and annual reviews and revisions of your plan, as needed.

Let's break it down a little further...

The Personal Strategic Foundation

Positive growth requires a solid foundation, just as a garden requires well-tilled and fertilized soil to support a successful harvest; or a contractor building a house needs to make sure to start with a level and firm foundation; so it is for a life well lived. To grow and truly live a life of direction, purpose and integrity, the key is to first define your Personal Strategic Foundation. This foundation consists of three things:

- **A set of personal vision statements** that describe, in vivid detail, the life you desire. They paint a clear and compelling picture of your life - *at some point in the future* - that you can visualize. At a minimum, there are statements describing your financial situation, your work, profession or business, your relationships with your significant-other, family and friends, your health and other personal areas such as your spiritual alignment and relationships within your community. These statements provide the guiding path to what you truly want for your future, the focus and direction for your daily efforts, and the compelling emotional drive for success.

- **A personal mission statement** that defines what you do, how you do it and for whom, and how you ultimately create value in the world. It defines your *unique purpose* which gives your life meaning and focuses your daily actions. Finding your unique purpose is a highly rewarding journey of self discovery that explores the natural gifts you bring to this world. Your inherent gifts can be found by exploring and understanding your given set of strengths, personality, learning style and how you are naturally motivated. As your gifts are understood, your unique purpose begins to be revealed, allowing you to define your personal mission statement. The personal mission statement creates a clear definition of the purpose of your life and answers, at least in part, the proverbial question, *"Why am I here?"*

- **Personal values** are simply a set of unbreakable rules you create to help you make decisions and live your life. With a clear and defined (written) set of personal values you will know what to do, (or perhaps more importantly, what not to do), and you will know how to figure out what you need to do to get where you want to go!

Together, your vision statements, your mission, and your core values define and form the foundation on which to build your life. They create a level, rock-solid base for building a life of direction, purpose and integrity. They provide the framework on which to build and execute a plan for your life because they give you a true and compelling direction (vision), a clear purpose (mission) and a set of values for staying true to yourself along the way (integrity).

The goal in developing your Personal Strategic Foundation, which we begin to discuss in greater detail on page 67, is to create clarity in your life. To focus on what is important to YOU and what is in true alignment with who you are, deep down. The goal is, literally, to de-clutter your life and get to your true essence.

Most people have some sense of what they want and wish to be. What they need is a process to help them determine, without a doubt, the right choices for them out of the hundreds of choices they encounter every day.

To begin to understand your own desires more deeply, we include a simple test here that we discovered in our research, as created and used by R. N. Remen, MD.[1]

Below you will find a list of 15 words which are common goals or desired outcomes people usually want in their professions and their lives. The test is to examine how we view the listed desires from these two aspects.

- First, list the following words in order of importance according to what is most important to you in your *professional life*, with the least important on the bottom.

Accomplishment	Adventure	Approval
Comfort	Fame	Friendship
Influence	Kindness	Love
Meaning	Money	Power
Respect	Security	Wisdom

- Second, do it again, but this time, list the words according to what is most important to you in your *personal life* with the least important on the bottom.

If you are like 90% of the people who completed this test for Dr. Remen, you came up with two different lists. Does it surprise you to discover that you think one way at

---

1 Remen MD, R. N., (2005) Health, Happiness, and the Well-Lived Life: A Doctor's Perspective, In *Live Your Best Life; A Treasury of Wisdom, Wit, Advice, Interviews, and Inspiration from O, The Oprah Magazine*, Birmingham, AL, Oxmoor House, p 80.

work and a different way in your personal life? Is your work life violating, or causing compromise in your personal life, or the other way around?

This is the power of a written Personal Strategic Foundation. When it is clearly defined and written, you will work toward alignment and integration between all aspects of your life and you can, perhaps for the first time, live in true balance, or what we refer to as successful work-life integration.

In addition, with a clearly defined Personal Strategic Foundation, thousands of potential choices or decisions (that you may feel need to be made right now) simply go away, leaving you with only a few simple questions to answer when faced with any decision: *"Is this option in alignment with who I am (my values)?"* *"Is this option in alignment with where I want to go (my vision)?"* *"Is this option in alignment with my unique value to the world (my personal mission)?"*

That's it! If something doesn't align, you can quickly discard it and not give it another thought. Can you begin to feel the POWER of that simplicity in your life?

Your Current State Assessment

Before you can effectively build an action plan to achieve your vision, activate on your mission, and live your values, you need to know where you are right now – your starting point. Your starting point is determined by assessing where you are today against the components of your Personal Strategic Foundation. Beginning on page 205, we provide a simple, easy, and highly effective assessment tool for determining where you are, and what it will take for you to *Live from Strength* each and every day. You will be able to use this assessment, and we encourage you to do so, over and over again anytime you need to refresh or re-align yourself to get back on your defined course.

The assessment will help you determine where you are and it will help you determine what changes or steps are needed so you can LIVE the life of your dreams. We will also show you how to prioritize the assessment so your annual action plan is focused on *first things first* and what is truly important and critical to you right now!

Your Personal Annual Action Plan

Once you have a foundation in place that provides direction, purpose, and values, and you have determined your starting point and prioritized your focus, you now need to take action to progress toward your vision and *activate* on your mission. In short, you need an *action plan*.

But first, let's dissect *action planning* down to its lowest common denominators – TODAY and the DECISION IN FRONT OF YOU in this moment! That's it! That is all you really have. When it comes to action, it is all about what you plan to do TODAY and what you are going to do with any given decision. We can't actually work in the future, nor can we change the past. Today, this moment, is all we have to work with, and when you think about it like that, *action* becomes easy because it happens - right now!

In that regard, any "plan of action" must help you figure out what actions you need to take TODAY to achieve your vision and activate on your mission. The plan must boil things down so you can act confidently today knowing you are making decisions and taking steps in alignment with your authentic self that will most likely lead you to success as you define it.

Therefore, a comprehensive and effective annual action plan that continually moves you toward the life you desire must have the right components to drive daily action, as defined in the following list.

As you read through this list, it may feel like a long list that would take considerable time to implement. Actually, the opposite is true for two powerful reasons. First, using these processes will actually save you time as they focus your actions to help you eliminate costly trial and error time wasters. Second, once these actions become practiced and routine, they take little time to create, review, and revise, sometimes just minutes a day.

The components of a sound action plan as you *Live from Strength* include:

- **A theme for the year that creates FOCUS.** This is a fun and positive statement of intent for the year that helps you focus on the major concepts, ideas, or aspects of your life that you choose to work on during this planning cycle. It might be financial in nature, or building relationships, or aligning yourself to consistently live your values. We will talk more about defining focus through a Personal Mission Statement (beginning on page 187) and how to effectively prioritize (beginning on page 219), and get clear, really clear, about what is truly important to you in your life RIGHT NOW! Thus, setting an annual theme is a tool

A quick note about goals: Notice the context in which goals are discussed here; goals as setting milestones and defining action. Later in the book, we discuss a new way to view and use goals that takes the stigma, pressure, and "fear of failure" out of them. See page 244 for more details.

to help you focus your efforts in a given time period, (in this case, one year), on the most important things for your life, right now, as you define them. We guide you through the process to set your annual theme later in this book, beginning on page 243.

- **A set of major goals for the year that define ACTION.** Once your focus is defined through your theme, it is time to put in place your major milestones, goals, and objectives to define and measure progress and specify the exact actions needed. We will help you build meaningful goals and objectives into your plan that are limited and focused on your theme so you can develop detailed action plans for each. We talk more about goals beginning on page 244.

- **Accomplishment Plans focused over a short, manageable length of time (weekly):** Based on the theme and the actions noted in your *major goals,* we recommend developing a list of the things you want to accomplish within the coming week. This further focuses your action into a manageable and meaningful, bite-sized time period. One week provides you enough time to confidently schedule your time and accomplish significant chunks of work, but short enough to effectively control the time without fear of significant changes to the plan. What is important is the act of translating the annual action plan into manageable and achievable activities that need to be done – in a way that works best for you – and being able to effectively schedule your time to accomplish those things you identified. We discuss Weekly Accomplishments Lists in greater detail on page 257.

Focused Daily Action

It all comes down to today! Once you complete the process you will have a time-tested tool to help you take action every day. Actions based on your Weekly Accomplishments List, which are tied to your major objectives, which are focused on your annual theme. You will act with confidence each day on those identified activities most likely in alignment with who you are, that lead you in the direction most important for you to get you where you want to go. More information on daily action planning can be found beginning on page 262.

We will also show you how to use positive daily affirmations to support your plan. Living your life with purpose and taking confident action each and every day is challenging. It is a challenge, in no small part, because there may be old thought patterns, untrue beliefs and negative ideas in your head preventing you from making the positive changes in your life that you desire. Therefore, in addition to a Daily Action Plan, we also strongly recommend the use and practice of positive affirmations to help you change negative thought patterns into a positive force. Reviewing your positive affirmations daily will keep your vision and values in front of you; remind you to voice gratitude for all the good in your life; and prompt you to continue asking the universe for what you desire. We will help you develop specific daily affirmations that support the theme and goals for your annual plan as well as other aspects of your Personal Strategic Foundation. We provide more detail on using positive affirmations beginning on page 265.

Review, Revise, and Refresh

For this process to be a powerful and effective tool that will assist you throughout your life, it must have a way to periodically, and systematically review your progress, revise your plan as goals and milestones are met, and refresh it as you and things around you change.

Beginning on page 279 we show you how to review and revise your Personal Annual Action Plan to keep it fresh and up-to-date as you achieve success and reach for more. As importantly, we show you how to quickly and effectively get back on course whenever you feel out of sorts and a re-alignment is needed.

All of the components of *The Personal Growth Challenge*™ process, when connected together, are designed to funnel you into meaningful and purposeful action each day, keep you aligned and focused year in and year out, and give you the tools to continually review, revise and refresh your plan as you go. Let's take a look at the process again, now including all the components discussed...

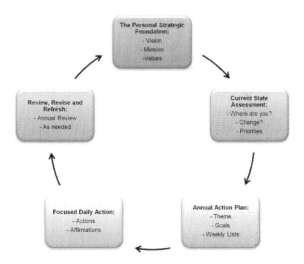

Figure 2: The Complete *Personal Growth Challenge*™ Process

As you can see, the *Personal Growth Challenge*™ process is truly a complete and comprehensive planning process for your life. Because it is so comprehensive, it may feel, at least at first glance, like a challenge. Well, of course it is! It is the most wonderful and glorious challenge you will ever face, the journey to YOURSELF, and we will guide you every step of the way!

In some of our recent readings, we discovered the *Personal Growth Challenge*™ process components also follow the principles outlined in the book *Living Deeply: The Art & Science of Transformation in Everyday Life* by Marilyn Mandala Schlitz, Ph. D., Cassandra Vieten, Ph. D., and Tina Amorok, Psy. D., with the Institute of Noetic Science.[2] *Living Deeply* is a culmination of years of research into the science of personal transformation which discovered four essential elements to a successful and long-lasting personal transformation (change), regardless of the person's practice (religious, pagan, Buddhist, etc.). These elements are:

- **Intention:** The intent, or personal choice, to change and transform.

For additional exercises and guidance and to join our online community of others experiencing The Personal Growth Challenge™*, visit our website at www.LivefromStrength.com.*

---

2 "Noetic" comes from the Greek word *nous*, which means "intuitive mind" or "inner knowing." For more information on the Institute of Noetic Science, visit www.noetic.org.

- **Attention**: Turning your focus and awareness toward what is needed to transform.

- **Repetition**: Practice. Like building strong muscles, the "muscles" of transformation need to be worked with repetition and practice of the "exercises" that will transform you.

- **Guidance**: Guidance and direction from experienced teachers and communities that help you stay on track and continually reach higher.

Thus, *The Personal Growth Challenge*™ process also contains all the needed elements for positive change, supported and backed by research and information from some of the best minds in personal transformation. It will help you get to the place where you can act and feel confident each day, awash in the belief that the actions you are taking right now are the most important to you as you create and live the life of your dreams. In addition, you will *know* the daily decisions you are making are in alignment with who you are, no more guessing! Your personal action plan turns the disciplined thought behind your strategic foundation into clearly defined actions that allows you to *Live from Strength!*

Summarizing Living from Strength

To Live from Strength comes from knowing that the actions you are taking TODAY are those that will most likely lead to success, as you define it. It comes from having built a solid personal foundation that defines who you are, where you are going, and how you want to live your life. This allows you to act with confidence, with purpose, and with intent to not just dream about, but truly LIVE the life of your dreams, one day, one decision, and one moment at a time.

Think about this incredible POWER for a minute... You have the ability to go beyond just dreaming and wishing for the life you want. You are now acting intentionally, confidently, and purposefully each day, each decision, and each moment of your life and actually LIVING the life of your dreams right now!

Take the *Personal Growth Challenge*™ process to heart and allow yourself to use the principles outlined. In return, you will experience success as you define it. It will be the most wonderfully rewarding challenge you will ever face! And if you have read this far you probably now believe, if you did not already, that the alternative of a complacent life is no longer acceptable.

Once again, if you can't wait to get started on your *Personal Growth Challenge*™ journey, feel free to skip ahead to Section I to begin developing your Personal Strategic Foundation. In the next chapter, however, we will give you some helpful tips for using this book so you can get the most out of the process.

How to Use this Book

This book is intended to be read through carefully, thoughtfully, and the exercises completed as you read them, and put into daily practice. We like to call it a "chewy" book; you take a bite and chew on it for awhile... savoring every tasty morsel. Though you will get a great deal of valuable information and keys to success if you simply read through it once, the real value is in going through the exercises, doing the work to define the life you desire, continually practicing the principles learned, and using the tools provided throughout your entire life. The process we teach, the *Personal Growth Challenge*™, is both a way to define your life - *and a way of life* where you live each day with purpose, direction, and integrity, and act each day with confidence to achieve what you truly desire. A way of life where you purposefully and intentionally live your dreams, each and every day!

In Section I, we start by creating a Personal Strategic Foundation that will define your purpose, direction, and focus. This Personal Strategic Foundation includes:

- A defined **vision** of your life that creates direction and compels you to action;

- A clear purpose or **mission** that gives your life meaning and focuses your actions each day;

- A set of unwavering **values** that guide and direct your decisions.

The development of the Personal Strategic Foundation will form the bulk of the work in this process and create the necessary context for planning your life. The Personal Strategic Foundation is a clear, concise, complete and - most importantly - a TRUE definition of you. This true definition of yourself is what makes your Personal Strategic Foundation incredibly powerful and amazingly motivating! A well defined foundation gives you the tools and the confidence to make the daily decisions that are right for you.

With this foundation in place, you now have the context to evaluate and put into practice the great success principles you learn from others - in a way that resonates with you. You will be able to understand which principles fit your life and quickly discard the ones that are not in alignment with you. You will find the confidence to act each day to do the things that will most likely lead to your success, as you define it. As importantly, this foundation will give you the freedom and power to manage positive change in your life. It will empower you to live in alignment with who you are, unleashing your strengths and true gifts, so you can BE all you are meant to be!

Next, in Section II, we provide you with a simple yet very effective way to *assess where you are today* against your personal foundation. This tool will help you see the many things already in alignment in your life and identify those areas that need additional focus. It will provide a way for you to clearly prioritize the areas needing work, but as importantly, it will clearly define your strengths and what you have already accomplished that can be capitalized on for even greater improvement and growth.

Once you know where you are today and where you want to go, we help you *put your desires into action.* In Section III, we guide you to focus your actions by setting meaningful goals and we teach you how to take action each day, with confidence, knowing you are doing things in alignment with your true self.

Many self-help concepts today talk a lot about secret laws and envisioning your dreams, but you cannot achieve your desires by simply wishing them to you. The missing key in that scenario is *action.* You must combine action with your dreams in order to move toward your desires. In Section III we show you how to build your Personal Annual Action Plan for your life, and how to execute (act on) that plan daily.

The result of going through the *Personal Growth Challenge*™ process defined in *Live from Strength* is the development of a simple and powerful set of tools you can use over and over again to create and manage your life. You will be able to continually update and improve your plan as you reach your goals and set new ones, as life changes around you, and as you change and grow.

The true power of the *Personal Growth Challenge*™ process is that it can be repeated over and over. You can go back and refresh any part of it at any time, or choose to go through the entire process again. You can even use it as an annual planning tool to keep you motivated and on track. You will also learn how to *update and maintain your plan* and how to realign yourself when you feel off target and out of sorts. The *Personal Growth Challenge*™ process is a valuable life tool that you will use every day to live your best life to its fullest.

Tips for the Journey

Before you begin this rewarding life-changing process, here are a few useful tips for your journey:

- You may feel a little overwhelmed at first after reading through the contents of this book and may even have a few concerns about the time it will take to go through each exercise. As with learning anything new, like studying a foreign language, starting a new job, learning a new dance style, or changing your golf swing, learning something new is an investment in *living* your life and it takes time. Pretty soon, however, after practicing that new dance step, you won't even think about your feet anymore – you just dance! And the return on your investment… *priceless!* So too you will find the investment of time in the *Personal Growth Challenge*™.

- We encourage you to take your time with every exercise as you work your way through the book. Plan to set aside one hour a week and move through the process at your own pace. That is all it takes to develop your plan to *Live from Strength* for the first time. You will find this hour (or more if you like) to be the most rewarding and compelling hour you spend with yourself each week.

- Once the initial plan is complete and you are comfortable with the tools we provide for LIVING the life you desire, you will need as little as 15 minutes a week to plan your weekly activities, and as little as five minutes a day to prepare and plan for the day.

- We also encourage you to set aside one-half day each year to review, update, and refresh your annual plan. Though it will take focused time to develop your initial plan, the beauty of the *Personal Growth Challenge*™ process is that once complete, it takes little time to revise and refresh and it provides you with a valuable tool to re-visit and re-group later when needed.

- If you have a computer and you normally work best by typing and managing electronic files:

  - Create an electronic file folder called "My Personal Growth Challenge." This is where you will save all of your exercises, drafts, and final copies.

  - For each exercise, create a new file with the title of each of the major documents you will produce. This includes: Personal Vision, Personal Values, Mission Statement, Personal Profile, Assessments, and Personal Annual Action Plan.

  - Develop a versioning system for your files that works best for you, such as "draft 1, draft 2, ... Final" or "V1, V2, ... VFinal," etc., so you can keep track of the various drafts and periodic updates that will occur. Using dates for versioning will help you keep your records in order year after year (Example: VFinalQ1-2013, for your final version for the first quarter of 2013.).

  - Print out your latest versions and have them with you - at all times. Keep them readily available for quick reference any time you need them. You can put them in your day planner or create a version to carry with you in your smart phone, notebook computer, or other hand-held device.

  - We recommend you use a spiral notebook to write and maintain your Weekly Accomplishments Lists and Daily Action Plans, but these can also be done electronically if that works best for you. Many electronic calendar and productivity tools have a "To Do List" functionality that can be used to manage your action planning. The point is to have a way to refer to your task list easily, quickly, and whenever you need. They should be at the ready at all times.

- If you do not have or use a computer...

  - Purchase a three ring binder and dividers and label the binder "My Personal Growth Challenge."

  - Label the dividers Vision, Values, Mission, Personal Profile, Assessments and Personal Annual Action Plan, for each of the major documents you will produce throughout the process.

  - Place your hand written versions in the binder and organize them so the most recent version is always on top.

  - Keep your three ring binder, or copies of the latest versions, with you - at all times - so they are readily available for reference when needed.

  - We recommend you use a spiral notebook to write and maintain your Weekly Accomplishments Lists and Daily Action Plans, if that works best for you.

    The point is having a way to refer to your task list easily, quickly, and whenever you need. They should be at the ready at all times.

- Throughout this book are various exercises and assessments we developed to help you *Live from Strength.* You can download, for free, all of the exercises exclusively developed for *Live from Strength* from our website at *www.LivefromStrength.com.*

An Important Note

The exercises and assessments throughout this book are intended to give you a general sense of your inherent strengths and natural abilities to help you better understand who you are and what makes you, you. Though a few of our assessments are mentioned in the context of noted authors, scientists, and scholars whose work has been scientifically validated, the exercises and assessments we provide here are not validated through scientific research. We have used these exercises in our practice for years, however, with great success, as measured by our client's positive acceptance of the results as a true and accurate portrait of who they are. Thus, we believe you will achieve similar results.

Where applicable, we have cited and indicated the scientific basis for our exercises and noted how you can acquire or take other tests that will give you scientifically-supported results if that is what you desire. Finally, all of the exercises and assessments in this book have been developed exclusively by us for our *Live from Strength* program, to include the *Personal Growth Challenge*™ process and should not be considered to represent the research or work of those authors, scientists and scholars referenced or cited herein.

It's About Time!

It's time to consider more fully each component of the Personal Strategic Foundation and how implementing these components into your life will save you time.

A couple of notes about time as we begin:

- Developing your Personal Strategic Foundation takes time. As we mentioned earlier in the book, how much time depends on you. Our coaching clients find it takes them an hour or so of focused time every week to complete each exercise to build their foundation within two to three months. They have also found these hours to be the most rewarding time they have ever spent. Time to focus on and, for the first time, truly plan their life. So to create meaningful results, plan to spend an hour or two each week on the exercises, give them your best effort, and expect that within a few months, you too will have defined your Personal Strategic Foundation.

- The beauty of creating a Personal Strategic Foundation is that, once defined, you will save an enormous amount of time over your lifetime. You will find you have more time to spend on all the things you want to do in your life, decisions will come easier, you will feel happier and at ease, and confident that your actions today are taking you where you want to go. Consider this process a valuable and cherished investment in your life; you are worth the time!

- Developing your Personal Strategic Foundation for the first time, though simple in concept, will take focus and effort. It can be a challenge (hence, why this process is called the *Personal Growth Challenge*™). It takes thought, introspection and, perhaps, courage, to do it. But this will be the most rewarding time and the most important effort you will ever make in your life for yourself.

- And once complete, you will find that you have just begun a new, exciting and rewarding journey. This is a continual, life-long process, one that we recommend you revisit at least annually and refine periodically. You will want to refine, revise, and renew your Personal Strategic Foundation often and whenever you feel it is needed. It is as ever flowing and ever changing as you are, and it is meant to change and grow with you!

Now it is time to begin this exciting challenge and venture deep into yourself to define your Personal Strategic Foundation, beginning with your personal vision.

Section I: Building a Personal Strategic Foundation

"All men can see these tactics whereby I conquer, but what none can see is the strategy out of which victory is evolved".
Sun Tzu

"Destiny is not a matter of chance, but of choice. Not something to wish for, but to attain."
William Jennings Bryan

The Power of a Compelling Vision

"If one advances confidently in the direction of his dreams, and endeavors to live the life which he has imagined, he will meet with success unexpected in common hours."
Henry David Thoreau

"Strategic planning is worthless – unless there is first a strategic vision."
John Naisbitt

You may have heard these quotes in your lifetime. Here are a few more... "If you don't know where you're going, any road will take you there." (George Harrison). Or, "If you don't know where you're going, you will wind up somewhere else!" (Yogi Berra). We like these quirky little quotes because they capture the essence of what happens when you are not in the driver's seat, actively navigating your life, and touches on what power is available to you by honing a clear focus, choosing a direction in alignment with who you are, and creating a compelling vision for achieving your dreams.

We all have desires, but how do we turn them into reality if those desires are not clearly defined and naturally motivating? Simply saying you want a successful business, a meaningful life, or a great relationship without clearly defining what that means to you is like saying, "*I am going to take the vacation of my dreams,*" but not specifying where you are going to go. How can you possibly get there if the destination is unknown? Why go through the trouble of planning a vacation without the destination in mind? It's also not enough to say, "*I'm going to the beach!*" Which beach? When and with whom? How will you choose to spend your time when you get there? To manifest the vacation of your dreams so you can live the experience, your vision of it must be crystal clear.

The same philosophy holds true with your life. Your life must also be clearly defined so you can get where you want to go. It's sad to think most people spend more time planning a vacation than they do planning their lives. Yes, it's satisfying to take a great vacation every now and then, but wouldn't it be more satisfying and rewarding to plan and live the life of your dreams EVERY DAY and take fun-filled, well-earned, guilt-free and truly fulfilling vacations that support that life?

Take a moment now to consider the following questions with regard to what you desire in your personal life:

What does your ideal health and well-being look like? What is your vocation, income, and net worth? Where do you live and how? What types and quality of relationships (with others and the world around you) do you have? And if you're looking for the relationship of your dreams, what does that look like? If you are already in a great relationship, how will you maintain and nurture its growth? Are you acting each day with confidence to achieve, create or maintain this ideal view of yourself and your relationships? If not, what ARE you doing?

Creating a Personal Vision of your life and your relationships, therefore, is foundational and one of the cornerstones to finding integration in your life so you can enjoy the journey. A Personal Vision is a clear, comprehensive, compelling and written picture of your life's many facets - *at some point in the future*. This is the target, or the "to be" view of what you really want in all aspects of your life. Let's look at this a little more closely:

- For a Personal Vision to be **clear**, we mean just that! Absolutely, unambiguously, and without a doubt clear, leaving you completely confident that your vision is *your* true desire and no one else's. A clear vision is also *focused*. It is your mental picture of a point in the future that has been boiled down to its very essence and separates what is absolutely important to you from your general day-to-day "to do" list (i.e., take out the trash, my turn to drive the car pool, finish that report at work, etc.). It contains only those things that, at the end of your life, you would want to be able to say, "*I accomplished what I set out to do.*" For example: I obtained my Master's Degree, ran a 10K with my daughter, wrote my memoirs, had deep and meaningful relationships, learned to dance tango, built a successful company based on integrity and passion that made a difference to the families of my employees and within the community, etc.

- **Comprehensive** means it involves every aspect of your life that is important to you. It leaves no stone unturned and ensures nothing truly important to you is missing. Looking at yourself as a whole, rather than in parts, helps you create and maintain an effective balance in your life that works for you.

- By **compelling**, we mean it touches you emotionally and draws, compels, and motivates you to *act*. It naturally moves you to action toward your desires. To create a compelling vision, you need to understand what you want, and why you want it.

- And, of course, to be truly valuable, your vision must be **written**. Writing your vision (in ink, pencil, crayon, visually on a vision board, or digitally recorded) is incredibly powerful, and along with reading, viewing or listening to it often, makes it real to you, not just imagined! Having it in a medium that works best for you makes it accessible and real. We recommend reading, viewing or listening to your Personal Vision daily, but certainly at least once a week.

Keep in mind, however, visioning is not a one-time process. Your Personal Vision is a living, breathing description of your desires that grows with you as you continue to define what you truly desire based on what you know today. It can and should be revised and updated often as your life changes and as you accomplish parts of your vision and set new directions. We recommend at least a three-year *look into the future* as you create and revise your vision. It is also important to update your Personal Vision each year as part of your annual life planning process, which we will discuss in more detail beginning on page 279.

A Clear Vision = Real Choice + True Power

You might be wondering now what a clear, comprehensive, and compelling vision can do for you. You will be amazed! A clear vision creates your direction and funnels your focus and in doing so, creates choice and power. Narrowing your focus may seem contradictory to having more choice, but it is not. Some people believe that choosing ONE direction in their life will limit their options and power of choice. Actually, if you think about it in this context, without clarity, EVERYTHING may seem like an option, or feel like the right choice, and so many choices can be exhausting and overwhelming causing you to stay where you are – stuck in a rut. That scenario actually limits your power, clouds your choices and puts roadblocks in the path to your goals! Once you have clarity of direction, however, you begin to see a clear path to your dreams. With clarity of direction, you are now attuned to the choices that are *right* for you. A world of possibilities opens up to you because you know exactly where you are going. A clear vision, in reality, empowers you to make knowledgeable choices aligned to your true desires. **This is real power and choice; the power to confidently choose the path that is right for you!**

Once you define your vision, you will likely experience serendipity. This is when you think about something and suddenly it walks right in the door. Opportunities will seem to pop up magically! We've seen it time and time again. But it's not magic. The scientific term is called the "reticular activating system," or RAS.[3] You know how this works... You buy a yellow car because you want your new car to be different from others, and all of a sudden you see yellow cars everywhere! They were there before, but you were not attuned to them. This is exactly what happens when you define a clear vision. All of a sudden you can see the answers you have been seeking. They were there before, but you were not focused and paying attention to them for what they could achieve for you. Knowing where you are going is real choice and true power!

Serendipity - 1) an aptitude for making desirable discoveries by accident. 2) good fortune; luck.

---

3 For more information and links to studies on the RAS, see
http://psychology.wikia.com/wiki/Reticular_activating_system.

Creating a Personal Vision

The process of creating a clear vision begins with dreaming about the life you really want. It is dreaming without bounds. In creating a vision, the only thing that matters is your deepest dreams and desires manifested in your thoughts and transposed to either the written or spoken word, visual images, or some combination. Dream as if the path to your desires is open, free and clear, that money is provided to you in abundance, and that all your relationships are positive and supportive. Think way outside of the box and believe *anything* is possible. Close your eyes, imagine – then express it in words or pictures.

Focus on what you want and deeply desire. Likely, you have "known" what you want your life to be like for some time. You probably have thought about it many times and dismissed this view because of perceived obstacles or road blocks. Now is the time to **allow** yourself to dream like you did as a child, and get those thoughts, dreams, and desires out of your head so they have real power! You will paint them with a brush of reality later in this process, but for now, it is time to dream, so dream BIG!

Although some believe that we are the sum total of our thoughts and experiences to this point, it is equally true that the past does not need to, and (in fact) cannot impact the present or the future, and certainly not your future vision, unless you allow it. You can DO and BECOME anything you want, regardless of your past. The reality may be that, because of your past, you may have more to overcome or you may have to work a bit harder or longer, but there are no real limits on your future except those that are self-imposed. As Napoleon Hill, author of *Think and Grow Rich,* stated, *"Whatever the mind can conceive and believe, it can achieve."* This has been proven time and time again by many people just like you.

Let's think about this quote for a few minutes. Really allow its meaning to sink in, *"Whatever the mind can conceive and believe, it can achieve."* It simply means if you can dream it up and believe you can achieve it, you can have it! That is the power of a clearly defined vision. It sets the ground work for finding the belief in yourself to achieve anything you want. We know it sounds cliché, but there really are no limits to your future except those you put on yourself. So, dream without limits... Dream as though your life depends on it, because it does!

Personal Vision Components

There are at least seven components of your life to consider when developing a Personal Vision. The components are listed on the following page in no particular order and the order they are listed does not imply any one to be more or less important. When you evaluate and prioritize your personal vision, discussed in more detail on page 219, you will be able to rank these components by their importance to you. For now, it is critical to explore and consider each of them equally so as to define the balance and integration between all the components that is right for you.

Tip: When you consider each component, focus on how you desire them "to be," not on how they are today:

- **Your Relationships:** Think about your relationships with family and friends. How is the relationship with your spouse or significant other? How about your kids? Siblings? Other family members? Friends? Remember, as we mentioned earlier in the book, what would you want your friends to say about you at your funeral? Think about that. When it is all said and done, how do you want to be remembered? A great person, a loving spouse, a wonderful parent, a terrific boss or co-worker?

- **Recreational Time:** Now focus on your free time. What are you doing with family and friends? What are you doing when you are alone? What are your hobbies? Describe your ideal and routine vacations? Is there something you've always wanted to try like dancing, acting, writing, hang-gliding, or kayaking?

- **Physical Health:** What is the condition of your body? Are you energetic and the picture of health? Are you physically fit? How often do you exercise? What do you do for exercise? What about your diet? What is it like? How do you feel about your ideal body?

- **Personal Areas:** Will you go back to school? Will you get additional training or certifications? Will you learn to play an instrument, speak Spanish, or take art classes? Where are you spiritually, and what role does spirituality play in your life? Do you desire to overcome or heal a past hurt? Do you desire to write a novel or publish an article in a respected magazine? How and where will you challenge yourself to grow personally and spiritually? What is the state of your emotional health?

- **Financial:** Think about the financial areas of your life. What is your annual income? How much money do you have in savings? What kind of investments do you own and how much are they worth? What is your total net worth? Create a clear, detailed picture of the home and possessions you have and explain why they are important to you. Remember, money is rarely, in and of itself, a true and real objective; however what that money can BUY (in terms of personal choice, satisfaction, and security) is what truly motivates us. So what does that look like for you?

- **Your Career or Business:** Visualize success in your career. Where are you working? Who are you working for, or with whom are you working? Do you own a business? What type? How much time do you spend in your profession? And of great importance, what value do you or your business in general, provide to the world? With whom do you do business and what are your clients like? How do they feel about you and the value of your services?

- **Community:** What does your relationship with your community look like? Are you involved in causes? If so, what are they? What community activities, clubs, charities or associations are you active and involved in? If your community was operating perfectly, what would it look like and what would be your role in making that happen?

Though these are the seven areas we believe everyone should consider in their Personal Vision, you may have other areas in your life that are also important to you, or you may choose to break down this list differently. That is OK, provided that you cover at least these items and that the resulting Personal Vision is crystal clear, comprehensive, compelling, and expressed in writing or visually in a way that resonates with you.

The Personal Vision Exercise

To develop your Personal Vision, you simply pick a date three or more years in the future. You then consider all of the components discussed above, and any others you may think of, and begin describing your life at that time in the future. That is it!

Like many things we cover in this book, the concept is simple, but the *doing* may be a little more challenging. In fact, most of our clients find this exercise the MOST challenging and exhilarating. Why? Because most of us have never really allowed ourselves to dream *without bounds*, without the shackles of the past, or without thinking of someone else first (like your kids, your spouse, your parents, etc.). Others have a hard time getting past "how." They may want something in their life but are unable to see how to make it happen so they let it go. When you're not used to thinking about *only* yourself, or dreaming without bounds and letting go of the "how," going through this lesson can be challenging. The result, however, if you allow yourself to dream, can be a very awakening time for you and provide some of the most amazing moments you will experience throughout this process.

Example Set of Vision Statements

Below, is an example set of vision statements. Mary is 42 years old. She has been married to Mark for 15 years and they have two children, ages 12 (Jack), and eight (Simone). Mary recently returned to work three years ago when her youngest started kindergarten. She has a college education with an undergraduate degree in Sociology. With few jobs in social work and public health today, Mary has been working as an administrative assistant for an insurance company since rejoining the workforce. She is struggling to find the type of work that will be personally fulfilling over the long term as she and her husband raise their children and plan for retirement.

Using this vision exercise, Mary created the following vision statements for herself looking five years into the future.

My Personal Vision

- **Health**: I am at my ideal weight of 125 pounds. I am healthy and fit and I feel great about my appearance. I maintain my weight, fitness, and appearance by exercising four to five times per week, including walking, dance, and yoga.

- **Personal Areas**: I have completed my advanced degree in Public Administration and I am managing a non-profit organization as a Director, focused on helping children. My spirituality and belief in God keeps me grounded. I attend church regularly and give of my time to those in need through our church.

- **Relationships**: Mark and I have a trusting, intimate and loving relationship and I daily express my appreciation of him in a way **he** understands. Mark and I get away together at least once a month (date-night) where our only focus is on "us." I have a strong and close relationship with my children and always express my love and acceptance of them, no matter what their behavior. I call my parents and siblings weekly. My girlfriends and I get together at least quarterly and more often, if possible, for a girl's night out where we renew and refresh our friendship and support for one another.

- **Financial**: I am making over $75,000 per year in my Director role, and our combined net worth is $500,000 or more. I have saved over $200,000 for retirement.

Our home is comfortable and a place where family and friends gather often for holidays and parties.

- **Career or business**: I am the Director of a non-profit that focuses on helping disadvantaged children and young mothers. My co-workers see me as energetic, dedicated and strong in business, caring and compassionate about our cause, and fair and open minded in dealing with staff.

- **Recreation**: I live a balanced life. I plan and spend time renewing and rejuvenating myself through regular exercise, scheduled alone time, time spent with family and friends, and frequent weekend getaways. We enjoy a family weekend trip each month and take two planned family vacations each year. We routinely take time off at the holiday season to spend time with family and friends, and to give to those in need.

- **Community**: I give of my time to my church supporting the needs of women and disadvantaged children. As a family, we donate our time each holiday season to organizations that feed the poor.

Vision Tips and Techniques

Now, it's your turn! The following tips and techniques will help you develop and make your Personal Vision work for you.

- **Set aside uninterrupted time.** This exercise deserves your full attention. You are worth it! This is your future, your life we are talking about, so give yourself some quiet time where you can be alone with your thoughts and really dig deep!

- **Give yourself permission to dream.** This sounds so simple, doesn't it? Give yourself permission to dream and to be 100% selfish. Yes, we said it, and we'll say it again... 100% selfish! You need to allow your vision to be truly all about you, at least in this dreaming phase. All of us have the reality of family, current situations, etc., but there will be plenty of time for painting this vision with the brush of reality later. That is part of the refining process. For now, however, the most important thing is to allow yourself to let go, dream big, and dream YOUR dreams!

- **Use bullet points, or key words and phrases.** You might want to start by going through each of the seven areas and simply noting key words and phrases. There is no need to write a novel your first time through. Just jot down the first things that come to mind. You can go back and put everything into meaningful sentences later. Your first, *off the top of your head* thoughts are likely closest to your true desires.

- **"Write it" with pictures.** For many individuals, creating a visual picture of your life is the first step and then using words to describe what you "see." You can even create visuals for each element of your vision by creating a "vision board," if this is something that works for you. A vision board, as outlined in the book and movie, *The Secret*, by Rhonda Byrne, is a visual representation of your vision statements. Example: If you desire a six figure income or a certain net worth, find a picture of a pile of money, or create a mock-up bank statement showing your exact income or net worth goal. Do you desire great relationships? Find happy photos of yourself with friends and family, or pictures of happy, smiling people in a magazine that represents your vision and label the picture "great relationships" or "happy together," etc. This is a very powerful medium. In fact, a vision board played a huge role in how my wife, Deborah, and I found each other! Deborah clearly defined what it was she was looking for in a committed, life-long, loving relationship. She then found pictures that visually represented that vision for her, and created a colorful, vibrant vision board that she focused on every morning while on the treadmill. She was literally walking toward her stated vision every day! Opportunities presented themselves and six weeks later, after a 17 year search for Deborah, we met "the love of our life" (each other) and were married a year later.

- **Write your vision as if it has already happened.** When you write down your dreams, make them read as if they are already real. Rather than saying... *"In three years I will have a house on the water."* You would say... *"I live in a beautiful home overlooking the water."* The idea here is that when you read your written statements (and you will read them frequently), the mind will begin to actually believe them and, along with positive action, you will more effectively bring them about.

- **Say it in positive, affirming language.** Write your vision statements in positive, affirming language. Rather than writing, *"I would like to not be fat and weigh 125 pounds."* You would say, *"I am at my ideal weight of 125 pounds, and I look and feel terrific!"* Or, instead of, *"I will hopefully no longer be afraid of success."* You might say, *"I am positive and confident about my future, and I am highly successful."* The point here is to write your vision statements in a positive form and in language that affirms what you really want rather than inadvertently focusing on the very thing you don't want. For every disease, illness, problem or shortcoming you have, there is a positive and affirming positive opposite. Your job is to find that positive expression of what you really want and - *write it down!*

- **Avoid the dreaded "weasel words."** Most people's first vision draft is full of what we call "weasel words." *Will. Might. Hope. Like. Wish. Try. Strive...* Again, these are not positive and affirming words to use. These words are cheats, frauds, and weasels in the hen house! They rob you of your power. As an example, to say, *"I strive daily to be healthy and fit."* Well, you will forever be "striving" to get there rather than having it. Simply say instead, *"I am healthy and fit."* NOW you can believe it. The power is in believing you ARE! Look through the first draft of your vision for these words and similar expressions and change any weasel words to, "*I am*," and "*I have*," etc.

- **Remember, your vision is not carved in stone.** When you feel your initial draft is 80-90% complete, it's time to move on. Why? Because the remainder of the process will help you hone it further. In addition, your vision will be constantly and continually revised as life situations change and with each yearly planning cycle. So when you are just about there, move on. The rest of the work to develop your Personal Strategic Foundation and your annual action plan will likely fill in the blanks.

- **Keep it private, for now.** This is YOUR vision. It is not your spouse's, your kid's, your best friend's, or your mother's. So, keep it private until it is nearly complete. Why? Because even the most well-intended spouse or friend can unduly influence your dreams. This does not mean you won't ever share it. In fact, quite the opposite. Once your vision is complete, one of the best strategies in making it real IS to share it with everyone! But until you know it truly represents you and your dreams and not someone else's, it is best to keep it your own little secret.

- **It is OK to borrow.** If you can't seem to find the words to best describe what you want, or writing isn't one of your strengths, that is OK, just borrow from others or use pictures and graphics from other sources. Maybe you have a favorite song or book that is meaningful to you? Use a passage from it! Use it and modify it to fit your needs. It is OK as long as what is eventually written or pictured truly resonates and represents YOU!

- At this point, you might be unsure about *HOW* you will reach your vision, and that is perfectly OK as well and very understandable. But with a continued focus on your vision, the *how* will be revealed to you. This is the POWER of a clear and compelling vision; the universe WILL provide the *how* when the *what* is clear!

Putting Your Vision into Practice

After you have gone through the process and completed the exercise, here are some tips and techniques for putting your vision into practice:

- Write down or print your vision statements and carry them with you. You can write them on a card or a piece of paper, and carry them in your purse or wallet, in your appointment book, or save a digital copy to your computer or hand-held device. Whatever works best for you, but keep them with you for reference at all times.

- Make a practice of reviewing them daily, but at least weekly. We will teach you a method for planning your week later in the process (beginning on page 257) where you will include activities that will move you toward this vision in each week's plan.

- Begin thinking about how you would prioritize your vision. Which of your vision statements seem most important to you? Which are most urgent? Which have to be done before others can be achieved? As humans, it is easier for us to focus on one thing at a time (yes, we believe multitasking is a myth), so later in the process (beginning on page 219) we will teach you how to prioritize and focus your efforts.

- Begin thinking about how close or how far you are from having, living, or achieving each aspect of your vision. No matter how close or how far you are, you can rest easy and be assured that the path you define here will get you where you want to go. Part of choosing to *Live from Strength*™ is to accept where you are today, let go of the past, and build a plan of action to achieve all that you desire.

- Review and revise your vision statements regularly. Like all parts of your Personal Strategic Foundation, they are not carved in stone and you can and will adjust your statements over time as you grow, change, and reach your stated goals.

Once complete, you possess a valuable tool – your own Personal Vision. You now have a defined direction for your life, the life of your dreams. Perhaps for the first time, you know where you are going and you are beginning to feel compelled to take action to make it happen. Your Personal Vision is now clear to you and simply awaiting your daily action. In other words, your life is ready to be LIVED!

Values Provide a Moral Compass

"Your true character is revealed by the clarity of your convictions, the choices you make, and the promises you keep. Hold strongly to your principles and refuse to follow the currents of convenience. What you say and do defines who you are, and who you are, you are forever."
Unknown.

If a compelling vision creates direction for your life, then a set of values provides you with the moral compass to stay on course as you journey toward your vision. So, what are values? There are several definitions. We're not talking about the value of time and money, or the value of hard work. We're talking about your personal principles and standards, your important beliefs and ideals in which you have an emotional investment. Your core beliefs guide your attitude and motivate your actions. Core values exemplify what you know to your soul to be who you are and what you stand for. They are your uncompromising beliefs.

As an example, *"I am a man of my word, honest, sincere, and caring of others."* If this is your value statement, you would feel very uncomfortable working for a company that requires you to withhold pertinent information or make false statements to customers in order to strong-arm deals to hit corporate sales goals. Or, if this company offered you a sales job after you had been unemployed for six months and you sensed this was their way of doing business, having clearly defined values would make it easier for you to decline the offer and hold out for something that is more in alignment with your core beliefs. Living in alignment with your core values brings peace of mind, less stress, more robust mental and physical health, and many other positive benefits!

Roy Disney, co-founder and long-term chairman of the Walt Disney Company, said, *"It's not hard to make decisions when you know what your values are."* Clearly defined values create a personal compass that you can refer back to time and time again. This personal compass will help you make better decisions, keeping you on the path that is right for you so you can get where you want to go in the least amount of time and with the fewest self-created obstacles.

Take a moment to think back over the major decisions you made in your past. You have already found your way through many defining crossroads that radically changed the course of your life. In those moments, did you choose a knee-jerk reaction and have to live with the consequences of your actions? Or, did you take the time to hold those moments up to your values to quickly evaluate what was right for you, taking a more pro-active approach before making your decision to act? You will likely have many more crossroads to face in your lifetime. What guidelines do you currently have in place to help you decide with confidence, in that moment, which way to go?

In our practice we have found that many important decisions our clients face come down to choosing between a "potential moment of discomfort vs. an actual lifetime of regret." Here is what we mean. When we don't have clear values and a decision-making framework, we often create in our mind some potential discomfort we might face if we make a given decision. We may fear the unknown, we may fear conflict with someone or rejection. We may fear any range of negative emotions from someone; anger, annoyance, disregard, etc. We may fear having to "go it alone" or not being popular or accepted. The key here is that all of these fears are not necessarily REAL. They are things that MAY happen, yet our fear of them potentially happening stops us from making a decision, or we make no decision at all.

Often then, we spend a lifetime regretting that decision (or lack thereof), wishing we had made a different decision, wondering what life would be like today if only we had chosen differently. Thus, with a clear decision-making framework based on authentic parameters, we can reduce the discomfort of the choice plus, should we still feel discomfort, balance that against our values and vision of our best self to simply ask which choice is in alignment and whether the choice is worth the potential risk of that moment of discomfort. Most of our clients begin choosing the potential moment of discomfort because they see that even if that moment of discomfort is real, they would rather suffer that discomfort and live authentically than choose differently and regret not living authentically the rest of their lives. When our clients begin realizing this is the choice, they choose authenticity, even if it means a moment of discomfort. The alternative is no longer worth it!

There is a fantastic quote by Steven Covey we love to share, "*The ability to subordinate an impulse to a value is the essence of the pro-active person. Reactive people are driven by feelings, by circumstances, by conditions, by their environment. Pro-active people are driven by values – carefully thought about, selected, and internalized values.*"

Most of us believe we have a set of values, our own personal code of conduct we would never violate. Many of us believe in honesty and integrity, and various "mom-and-apple-pie" ideals. Some people aspire to live up to a set of values defined by their spiritual beliefs or religion. Others have developed their values through life experience. Some, through self reflection, discover their values were imposed on them by the teaching of their parents or church and have struggled through life because, down deep, they know these beliefs are not their own.

Few of us, however, actually take the time to consciously go through the process to clearly define and write our own *unique* set of values that resonate within ourselves. Consequently, when the going gets tough and we're backed up against a wall, we invariably waffle (react) and make some pretty bad choices along the way. These reactive "bad choices" cause us to take major detours we didn't expect, keeping us further from our intended destination. With a clearly defined (written) set of personal core values, you will simply know what to do; or, perhaps more importantly, what not to do. You will become a pro-active person!

Personal values are your unbreakable life rules. They are your ethical and moral compass on your life's journey. They form the foundation for all decision making and are constantly referred to and applied, whether consciously or not, in every decision-making process. Have you taken the time to clearly define yours?

You might believe your religion or spiritual orientation provides you with all of the guiding principles you need, and that may be true. For you then, the process of values development may be simple and quick, but the power of the results will be no less amazing. The power will come from distilling (or focusing) the teachings from your faith to those values which resonate with - and are most important to - *you*. Then, you will have in your hand a simple, clear, and definitive written list of guiding principles (your compass) representing your unique self that will most effectively guide you on your personal journey.

Imagine knowing you can face any challenge in life because you have the tools to make the decisions you know will be right for you. Imagine having the guiding principles at the ready to nearly instantly determine your true path time and time again. Powerful! And, it's all within you already!

If you desire to live your life with true *purpose and meaning* (a mission), you need a *clear direction* (a vision), and *a compass* (your written values) to keep you heading in the direction that's right for you. Once you have defined these three foundational principles, you will have the tools to create the action plan to achieve your dreams.

The Values Exercise

Our Values Exercise will help you clearly define your set of core values. The goal of this exercise is to develop three to 10 clearly written statements that form your most important values. Why only three to 10? Simple: One or two are too few and doesn't provide enough guidance, while having more than 10 doesn't provide enough focus. Most people develop between five and eight value statements through this exercise.

The process of defining your values begins by quickly reviewing dozens of words commonly thought by most people to be values in our society for which we aspire to in life and business. Rate each word as you read through the list. Most of them will have some importance and meaning to you, but there will be a few that stand out and strike you to be of utmost importance.

Herein lies the power... defining those values of utmost importance to you is *freeing*. Values defined - creates *clarity of who you are*. Clarity of who you are frees you from worrying about a hundred rules that don't really matter to you, or a thousand decisions you don't need to consider. You ONLY need to focus on those opportunities that are clearly in alignment with your focused values, making things seem, all of a sudden, not so overwhelming after all!

These defined values will become your *personal moral compass*, guiding your decisions on a day-to-day basis. They can be revised or adjusted as you grow and change, but never compromised. They are non-negotiable, indisputable, and tell everyone who you are and what you stand for.

Make a photocopy of the following four pages, or visit our website at *www.LivefromStrength.com* to print a free copy of this exercise (use the password "LiFSExercises" to access the files), and set aside some uninterrupted focus time (perhaps an hour or so) to complete the exercise. Let's begin!

Phase I: Values Identification

For each of the values listed on the next two pages, give a rating of either A, B or C where:

A = Absolutely critical and essential. These are required fundamental values that are of critical importance to you and essential for you to *Live from Strength*.

B = Important but not essential. These are important values that have a strong meaning for you, but you don't see them as absolutely essential for you to be able to *Live from Strength*.

C = Not important or only somewhat important. These are good values, but they are not that important to you and are not the values you believe are essential for you to *Live from Strength*.

Please add any other values you feel are missing from the list. After all, these are your values.

Go through the list rapidly. Your first thought for each word will likely be the right choice for you. You will have time later to evaluate your responses.

Ready? GO!

List of Values:

__ Abundance
__ Acceptance (of others)
__ Accomplishment
__ Accountability
__ Accuracy
__ Achievement
__ Aggressiveness
__ Appreciation
__ Attention to Detail
__ Challenge
__ Commitment
__ Communication
__ Community
__ Competitiveness
__ Concern for Environment
__ Concern for Others
__ Consensus
__ Continuous Improvement
__ Control
__ Courage
__ Credibility
__ Curiosity
__ Decisiveness
__ Discipline
__ Diversity
__ Education
__ Energy
__ Entrepreneurship
__ Equality
__ Excellence
__ Fairness

__ Faith
__ Family
__ Financial Freedom
__ Fiscal Control
__ Friendship
__ Fun
__ Generosity
__ Getting the Job Done
__ Goodness
__ Gratitude
__ Hard Work
__ Health
__ Honesty
__ Honor
__ Individual Initiative
__ Individualism
__ Innovation
__ Integrity
__ Justice
__ Leadership
__ Learning
__ Loyalty
__ Mentoring
__ Mobility
__ Money
__ Nurturing
__ Openness
__ Organization
__ Patriotism
__ Perfection
__ Performance
__ Persistence
__ Personal Growth
__ Personal Responsibility

__ Pleasure
__ Positive Attitude
__ Pride
__ Privacy
__ Prosperity
__ Purity
__ Quality
__ Reasonableness
__ Reliability
__ Resourcefulness
__ Respect
__ Responsibility
__ Responsiveness
__ Results
__ Risk Taking
__ Rule of Law
__ Security
__ Selflessness
__ Self-Reliance
__ Service (to others)
__ Sincerity
__ Skill
__ Spirituality
__ Stability
__ Status
__ Strength
__ Structure
__ Style
__ Systemization
__ Teamwork
__ Timeliness
__ Thriftiness
__ Togetherness
__ Tolerance

__ Tradition
__ Trust
__ Truthfulness
__ Value (to others)
__ Variety
__ Vision
__ Wealth
__ Well-Being
__ Other: _____
__ Other: _____
__ Other: _____

Phase II: Values Grouping

Once you have selected the values that are of utmost importance to you (those rated an "A"), on a separate piece of paper, move them into groups of words with similar meaning to you (such as "trust, honesty, integrity"). For example, the first word in your list of "A words" begins the first group. Now look at the second "A" ranked word in your list. If it feels like it belongs with the first, add it to that group. If not, it starts a second group. Now look at the third word. If it belongs with either group, add it there or start a new group. Continue this process until you have gone through all of the "A" ranked words in your list. You should have between three and 10 groupings when complete. You may also have a group of words that don't seem to fit in any of the other groups, simply list those separately.

Phase III: Values Definition

Once all the A's have been grouped together, identify the *overarching theme* for each group. For example, a group that has "honesty, integrity, and trust" might have a theme of "integrity" because that is the value that resonates most with you.

Now, using the other words in the group, create one statement or short paragraph that represents the group and provides a definition of what that means to you. For example: *"I live with integrity at all times. I am honest with everyone and trusting in them."* Another example, a group that has "loving, nurturing, family, fun, and structure" could be, *"I am a loving and nurturing parent to my children. I enjoy my family, value the structure we have created, and we have fun together."* If you have a group of words that don't seem to fit, review each word and ask yourself if it is truly important to you or whether it might "stand alone" as a value. If it is not of utmost important to you, discard it, at least for now. You will have ample opportunity to evaluate your values throughout the process. If the value is important to you, such as "Pride" and it seems to stand alone, write a value statement to describe what that word means to you.

Example Value Statements

Below is an example set of value statements for Mary, who we introduced during the visioning process on page 78.

My Personal Values

- My family is of upmost importance to me and I truly appreciate all the love, trust and respect they provide me.

- I am committed to excellence and decisiveness in my performance for all that I am responsible.

- I pride myself on being reliable and accountable for results.

- I approach life with energy and a positive attitude.

- I create balance in my life with a focus on my health and well-being.

- I am concerned for and committed to the service of others, especially children and those who are less fortunate.

- I make decisions that are fair and I am tolerant and respectful of the beliefs of others.

- I have a deep faith in God and practice my spirituality through my work with our church.

- Integrity is my hallmark and I communicate with honesty and truthfulness.

Putting Your Values into Practice

Now that you have completed the exercise, here are some tips and techniques for making your personal values work best for you:

- Write your values down and carry them with you. You can write them on a card or a piece of paper, and place them in your purse or wallet, in your daily calendar, or save a digital copy to your computer or hand-held device. Whatever works best for you, but keep them with you for reference at all times.

- Refer to them often and put them to the test. Put them into practice in your life and test their validity and resiliency. Actually refer to them and use them whenever you face a tough decision. Do they help? If not, ask yourself what is missing? If yes, how? Make adjustments where necessary and continue to refine your values until they feel absolutely right to you and stand the test of time.

- Begin thinking about which values you consistently live and those you do not. For those values newly formed, the ones you have yet to fully put into practice, determine whether living to them requires you to make significant changes in thoughts, feelings, and actions. Later in the process you will learn how to turn these values into positive affirmations that will help you change your thoughts, feelings, and behaviors to better align with the values you have now defined.

- Keep in mind, you may have to balance between values to stay true to yourself or balance one against another in a given situation. As an example, most people will have some form of value statement about truth and honesty and most will have some statement about valuing relationships with family and friends. Will you tell your best friend that you don't think her watercolor painting of a still life is very good (being honest), or are you going to say something nice for the good of the relationship? Will you live and hold true to your values concerning faith or religion, or will you live the value of being accepting of others even though they may be different from you? There is no wrong or right answer, only the answer that is most right for you!

- Review and revise your value statements regularly. Again, they are not carved in stone. And though they do not change with each situation (something we call "situational ethics"), they can adjust over time as you grow and change. Your value statements can and will be reviewed periodically and revised, as needed. As you test them, you may find holes in your values or find them too rigid or oppressive. Nothing says you have to get it right the first time. Life is a process, so make the needed adjustments and move forward.

- Forgive yourself if you violate your values. Odds are, at some point, you might. We are all human after all. So if you make a mistake, forgive yourself and resolve to do better next time. Just let it go and move on!

Once complete with this exercise, you now possess a second valuable tool – your own personal moral compass. Combined with your Personal Vision (the first tool), use these values to guide and shape your everyday choices.

So now, here is the challenge... Will you use your shiny new compass to navigate your life's journey or will you tuck it away in a drawer and forget about it? The choice is yours. Don't lose another moment of feeling certain that the steps you are taking are getting you closer to your dreams.

Purpose - The Personal Mission Statement

"When you discover your mission, you will feel its demand. It will fill you with enthusiasm and a burning desire to get to work on it."
W. Clement Stone

At one time or another, we all ask ourselves, *"Why am I here?"* Or, *"What is my purpose on this earth?"* Many are searching for the answers to these questions. Others never bother to try to answer them, believing no one really has a unique purpose in life.

The fact is, everyone has a purpose, and you know inherently it! You may not know WHAT it is, but you know it to your soul that there is a reason why you are here. Sadly, too few in our society are encouraged or taught how to find and define their personal mission so they can live their purpose every day. You likely know people, or know of people, who live with purpose in their lives. They are the ones who create extraordinary value in the world by living their truth. They have a clear understanding of what they bring to this world, who they serve, and the value they provide. Many know their purpose and act on it daily, but most of us need a little guidance to get there as well.

Thus, these are not rhetorical or theoretical questions, they are, in fact, the most important, real and challenging questions you will face in defining a life focused on who you really are. This is the true challenge – *The challenge to live a life of purpose, integrity, and intent, each and every day.*

Take some time now to think about, and write down or record the answers to these very real questions:

- If you could do anything you want for work, would you do what you are doing now? If not, what type of work would you do? Would you work indoors or outside? Would you write? Lecture? Think? Fix things? Build things? Invent things? Remember when you were a kid and you were asked, *"What do you want to be when you grow up?"* How did you answer that question then? Does that answer seem silly now, or does it still resonate with you in some way? You still have a lot more growing to do, so what would you do if you could do anything? Allow yourself to answer that childhood question now, *"What do you want to be when you grow up?"*

- If you could bring value to this world, what value would you bring? Would you educate others? Would you help feed the hungry in the world? Would you bring joy to people's lives and in what way? Aid those who suffer? Help those in need? Would you help create wealth or improve productivity and performance for others?

- If you could serve any group of people such as children, the elderly, adults, women, men, those suffering medically, those who are seeking answers, etc., who would you most like to serve? Would you serve individuals, businesses, or teams of people? Who would most value what you bring to the world?

These are the very questions that constitute the basis of a Personal Mission Statement.

A Personal Mission Statement clearly defines three things:

- **What you do.** This is the work you do that will take you where you want to go in your vision. It is the work that will give you satisfaction, meaning, and purpose in your life, one happy and contented day at a time.

- **Your unique value proposition.** This is the unique value you provide to the world. This is the result that people or organizations (which are simply larger groups of people) get from you or your efforts. It could be joy, wealth, information, knowledge, skills, a better life, etc.

- **Who you serve.** These are your customers. These are the people or organizations that most value your unique value proposition. This could be all people (everyone needs food, for example) or it could be very specific (caring for children with leukemia, or home schooling my children).

Creating a Personal Mission Statement is designed to provide you with the clarity of focus and direction in your vocation and align you to your passions and inherent strengths. It tells everyone you come in contact with if you can be of service and value to them and how. And it allows you to know, very quickly, whether you can be of service and value to those you encounter.

A Personal Mission Statement also helps you focus on providing value to the world so the world can then give back to you in abundance. Many people go through life thinking things like, *"If only they paid me more, I would do more (work harder, be more productive, etc.)."* Or they might say, *"If they give me that promotion, then I will show them what I can really do."* Or they might say, *"Why would anyone pay me to do what I love to do?"* But the world and the universal laws of attraction in which the world exists do not work that way. You must FIRST provide the world with value and then it will give back to you in valuable abundance.

A Personal Mission Statement is about giving up on outcome, which you cannot control, and focusing on freely giving of your talents and gifts to create real value, which you can control. You might be thinking, *"I'm certainly not going to work for free,"* and that is not what we are saying here. If you can clearly communicate the value of what you do, the world, and the people and companies in it, will see that value and pay you more than adequately.

A Personal Mission Statement also takes the focus off "making money" and focuses more appropriately on the value you provide. Money is a tool, it is not an objective. People may be highly motivated when they lack money, but according to most major studies in the area of motivation (notably Abraham Maslow's Hierarchy of Needs theory[4], Frederick Herzberg's "two-factor" theory[5], Marcus Buckingham and Curt Coffman of the Gallup Organization[6], and most recently Daniel Pink in his book *Drive*), money rarely is a long-term motivator for continued achievement in a work environment. Money buys us the things we need and making money alone is rarely personally fulfilling. What you do to earn the money and what that money can provide (such as peace of mind) is what can be personally fulfilling.

It does not matter where you are in your life, nor does it matter how capable you are at the moment of delivering on your mission statement. That can occur in the future. The Personal Mission Statement simply helps you create *focus* regarding the training, education, and career development necessary in order to *become* the person who can deliver on the mission.

---

4 A.H. Maslow, A Theory of Human Motivation, Psychological Review 50(4) (1943):370-96.
5 Herzberg, F., Mausner, B. & Snyderman, B.B. 1959, The Motivation to Work. John Wiley. New York.
6 Marcus Buckingham, First, Break All The Rules, 1999, Gallup Press.

So, how do you develop a Personal Mission Statement? How do you discover your true calling, your value, and who you will serve? Likely, deep down inside you have a feel for your "right answer," right now. You may have had a desire to do something since you were young or have always enjoyed certain types of work over others. For most people, that little voice inside has been telling you for years, perhaps all your life, but the rigors of life and self-doubt have somehow gotten in the way of exploring that dream.

Quite frankly, most of us have not learned how to sort through all those thoughts and feelings to get down to our essence. Most of us need to be shown how to categorize, prioritize, and separate our whimsical desires from those things that are in true alignment with who we are. We also need to understand the importance of separating our true strengths and unique gifts from our wishes and desires about who we want to be. (As an example, I may really want to play basketball like Michael Jordan, but I am not uniquely gifted to that task, nor am I uniquely gifted at creating original works of art.) It is also important to truly embrace our unique gifts as the tools we possess to create meaning and purpose in our life, and provide value to the world. We need to believe that we truly DO have powerful and meaningful gifts, and that focusing and developing them are foundational to our future success.

This is the essence of the *Live from Strength* process. This process requires you to honestly and deeply assess who you are. It will help you push away and get beyond the "maybes" and "only ifs" and get to the center of your authentic self. It will guide you to discover your unique gifts and build confidence in your ability to create and live the life you truly desire at any age through a Personal Mission Statement based on these gifts. The development of a Personal Mission Statement begins with understanding your *true self*.

Understanding Your True Self

No matter our chosen profession, and regardless of our upbringing, we all have a natural way of being and we know our "way of being" (in terms of personality, talents, capabilities, ways of communicating, and ways of being motivated) is different from those around us. We know from experience *when* we are in alignment with our natural way of being. We perform better, feel better, have more success, and we get outstanding results. We may not exactly know WHY we are in alignment, but we know when we are and when we are not. Thus, what we are attempting to do here is to help you clearly understand your natural way of being so that you can, with purpose and intent, stay in alignment with yourself and enjoy those positive feelings more consistently.

For the purposes of developing your Personal Mission Statement, and thus the focus of your life, there are three aspects of who you are (outlined below) that intertwine with your unique gifts and the value that you bring to the world. It is necessary to explore and understand these aspects of yourself in order to discover and develop a unique and meaningful purpose for your life:

- **Your *talents*.** These are your natural capabilities that can be honed with practice and skill to true mastery to become your unique strengths.

- **Your *learning style*.** This is the dominant way you process and communicate information.

- **Your *motivation style*.** This is the natural or intrinsic way in which you are motivated or compelled to action.

Together, these personal aspects provide you with a unique set of tools, your unique gifts that can be packaged and, in effect, sold to perspective "buyers." This could be employers who need those skills, or you can apply them to your own business and then directly to your customers, or you can share them with your family while you raise your children or care for aging parents. The unique combination of these aspects of ourselves makes each one of us a very unique individual. Thus, your Personal Mission Statement focuses your efforts each and every day so you can deliver your unique value to the world.

You can learn to do most anything but personal fulfillment and excellence come only when you are right aligned with your true self; your inherent talents, your unique learning style, and your intrinsic motivations. Can you be happy without that? Of course! Happiness is a choice, after all. But we are talking about true personal fulfillment and the ability to consistently perform at an extraordinarily high personal and professional level (what Daniel Pink calls **mastery**). That comes only when you are truly doing what you were meant to do in your life. And what you were meant to do is most likely found when you are in alignment with your unique gifts; your unique talents, learning style, and motivations.

The following three chapters will help you discover your natural talents, your learning style, and your motivation style. You will come to understand your unique strengths and corresponding weaknesses. You will also discover what very successful people already know – that only a focus on your strengths is deserving of your time and energy.

Understanding your learning style and how that impacts your communication style, will help you realize how both impact your unique purpose. By learning how you are naturally motivated, you will discover why you take action and get certain things done easily while other things seem more difficult to complete. Most importantly, you will learn how to align yourself to naturally take action and defuse de-motivating workplaces and activities.

Creating A Deeper Understanding of You

Doing the suggested work in the next three chapters will give you a new understanding and insight of what makes you, YOU; and it will provide the fundamentals needed to most effectively define your unique purpose and your Personal Mission Statement.

To assist you in putting all this information together into your first Personal Mission Statement we introduce you to the concept of the Personal Profile.

Your Personal Profile will list and describe your unique gifts; your strengths, natural learning style and intrinsic way of being motivated. You will describe how these are truly unique to you and how to use them in a positive way to get the most out of life. You will also explore how others might perceive you in a less than positive light when you take these gifts to extreme, and what you can do to manage these "perceived weaknesses."

The result is a powerful tool you can use over and over again throughout your life for continued refinement of your Personal Mission Statement as you develop a deeper understanding of yourself while living from strength.

Embracing Your Talents

"The road to happiness lies in two simple principles: find what it is that interests you and that you can do well, and when you find it put your whole soul into it - every bit of energy and ambition and natural ability you have."
John Rockefeller

"Each of us has been put on earth with the ability to do something well. We cheat ourselves and the world if we don't use that ability as best we can."
George Allen – Professional Football Coach

Based on the ground breaking work done by the Gallop International Research and Education Center, as detailed in the book *Now Discover Your Strengths* along with its prequel, *First, Break all the Rules*, authors Marcus Buckingham, Curt Coffman, and Donald Clifton define talents as *"your naturally recurring patterns of thought, feeling or behavior that can be productively applied."* They further explain, *"If you are naturally competitive, inquisitive, or persistent, these are talents."* So is being naturally charming and responsible, provided you can apply them productively.

What about being obstinate, irresponsible, or other widely considered negative traits? What about so-called disabilities, such as dyslexia? Could these also be talents? According to these authors, and according to the work we have done, the answer is a definite YES, provided they can be applied productively! In our practice, we have counseled people with interesting behaviors or challenging learning disabilities, who had always seen their personal situation as "limiting" factors, preventing them from their desired success. They realized, however, once they went through this process and learned to use these traits productively they were able to do some pretty remarkable things!

Remember Julia, the attorney we introduced to you earlier in the book? She's the one who saw herself as "quirky," and felt that these naturally occurring thoughts, feelings, and behaviors were not very "lawyerish." What she discovered, however, is those very different thoughts and feelings helped her find unique and creative solutions for her clients' problems. Thus, her traits that some might consider "negative" were actually a talent, and thus a great strength for her when applied productively. This discovery also allowed her to accept and love herself just the way she is, and understanding her strength made her feel more confident in her daily actions.

Another client, Greg L., discovered that his apparent "weakness" of being interested in so many things (perceived as an inability to focus and decide on a career) actually stemmed from his "strengths." Greg's passion is to learn "the new thing" and he has a strong ability and need to acquire data and information. Once he understood his perceived "weakness" only occurred when he took his strengths to extreme, he began to learn when to "pull back" on his needs in certain situations while at the same time learning to embrace his strengths and value them for what they could do when properly managed.

Understanding your talents, therefore, is the foundation to understanding your unique gifts which leads you to the creation of a unique value proposition; your unique value to the world. Your unique value proposition is the key to discovering your individual purpose (the way you provide your value to the world) that is defined by your Personal Mission Statement.

Once you discover your talents, you can develop your strengths. Yes, strengths must be developed with knowledge and skill. You do have to work at it, which is another part of this exciting challenge! Great athletes may have been born with innate talents, but the most naturally gifted are not all playing at the professional level. Only those with the dedication to develop those talents into strengths by learning and studying the game, and purposely developing their skill through practice, are playing professionally today. Those are the ones who make it to the highest level.

This is true in any profession. By first understanding your talents, your naturally occurring patterns of thought, feelings, and behaviors, you can develop them into strengths and most effectively and productively apply them to create a unique value proposition and find your unique purpose.

Discovering Your Talents

To begin to discover your unique talents, we have developed a simple exercise that will help you sort through the jobs and activities you have done in the past so you can begin to understand the unique attributes you brought to them. This exercise, however, is only the beginning of understanding your talents. Also, beginning on page 129, we will discuss a more comprehensive "strengths test" that we use in our practice and give you additional exercises to help you focus on your strengths and understand how those strengths may actually become your greatest weakness, when taken to extreme. Thus, no matter which way you look at it, developing your talents or conquering your weaknesses, it really comes down to a focus on your STRENGTHS!

Phase I: Identify the Work, Activities, and Tasks You Have Enjoyed

Take some time now to think back over your life and all of the jobs you have held and the work you have done. If you are younger, think back through your school experience. Also consider any volunteer activities, special assignments, tasks, or projects you worked on, on or off the job, in or out of school. Think about your hobbies and the things you do for recreation.

As you consider each of these things, make a list of the work, tasks, activities, or projects on a separate piece of paper where any of the following applied:

- You really enjoyed the tasks in your position.
- You felt particularly valued (by others) for your contribution.
- You felt you provided significant value (to others).
- You had fun doing it.
- You found the work or tasks easy.
- You woke up in the morning feeling excited about going to work.
- You came home with a feeling of satisfaction for a "job well done!"
- You felt energized by the work.

In general, you will list all the jobs, activities, or experiences where you felt a general alignment. It is likely that you enjoyed it, felt valued, or found it easy because you were "in your element" utilizing your strengths. Thus, identifying jobs you enjoyed is the first step toward discover your unique gifts. For some of us, however, we may have to look beyond the job to specific tasks or projects within the job. This is because the job itself may not bring joy, excitement or energy, and that is OK, as few people are lucky enough (though we call it "intentional enough") to be working in their dream job, but you likely have/had tasks in the job that you like doing more than others.

Phase II: Identify Exactly What You Were Doing

For each of the items on the list from Phase I, attempt to describe exactly what you were doing, or what you did that made it enjoyable, fun, valuable, energizing, etc. To assist you, we have compiled a list of the kinds of things you might have done and some conditions that may have made it a great job. Circle the ones that truly resonate and write the name of the job or task identified in Phase I next to it.

For example, you might have worked for a software company as a programmer. The work was OK, but one time you were asked to manage a project and really enjoyed it. So, in the following list below, you might circle: "I was in charge," "I was able to build meaningful relationships," and, "There were clear deadlines and guidelines." When you circle these, you would write "Project Manager" next to those circled items.

As another example, you may have volunteered at an organization for a project and the following might resonate with you... "I felt included in all aspects of the project," "I was recognized for my contributions," and, "I was able to make sure everyone was included." When you circle these, you would write "Volunteer" next to those circled items.

Feel free to add to the list if you do not find what you are looking for here.

IMPORTANT: Circle only those statements where you are sure they describe something you actually did, experienced, or felt. This exercise is not about how you WANT TO BE, this is an exercise to analyze what you have actually done and experienced. We find that most people have somewhere between 15 and 20 items on their list when complete.

Activities and Actions

- Building rapport and getting to know one another was an integral part of the job.

- Everyone had a chance to show what they could do.

- Everyone was treated equally.

- Goals were clearly defined and the tasks well understood.

- I felt included in all aspects of the project.

- I learned by doing.

- I made things happen.

- I took action.

- I was able to accomplish a lot.

- I was able to align or arrange many variables.

- I was able to analyze and review information and data.

- I was able to build meaningful relationships.

- I was able to challenge others to get the best from themselves.

- I was able to collect things and use them in the project.

- I was able to figure out how things were structured or formatted.

- I was able to get people to agree.

- I was able to help others develop, grow and succeed.

- I was able to learn a lot.

- I was able to make sure everyone was included.

- I was able to meet a lot of new people.

- I was able to restore something and make it shiny and new.

- I was able to see and explore the strengths

and differences of everyone on the team.

- I was able to solve problems and find solutions.

- I was able to sort through chaos and find the best path.

- I was able to take my time and really think things out.

- I was able to think and stretch my mind.

- I was allowed to be flexible.

- I was allowed to brainstorm and come up with new ideas.

- I was allowed to dream and be creative.

- I was allowed to figure out the best way to get things done.

- I was allowed to respond to the needs of the moment.

- I was an advocate for others.

- I was appreciated for having a thirst for knowledge.

- I was appreciated for taking responsibility.

- I was challenged.

- I was communicating.

- I was given the authority to act on my judgment.

- I was given time for thought and reflection.

- I was given time to get oriented.

- I was in a competition.

- I was in alignment with my values.

- I was in charge.

- I was involved in strategic discussions.

- I was judged on my performance and my performance alone.

- I was kept to strict guidelines and deadlines.

- I was not forced to settle for less than a great output.

- I was or felt connected to everyone involved.

- I was recognized for my contributions.

- I was the emotional lightning rod for the team, keeping everyone upbeat and positive.

- I was the visionary.

- I was truly appreciated for my unique gifts.

- I was writing, speaking, or hosting.

- I won awards.

- My candid nature was appreciated.

- My collection of great information was valued.

- My confident attitude in my abilities was appreciated.

- My job "stood for something" and had meaning.

- My positive spirit was appreciated.

- Others also took responsibility for their work, like me.

- People really cared about performing at a high level.

- People's differences were celebrated.

- The risks were known or discussed for everyone to see.

- There was a clear sense of history and drawing on the past.

- There was little conflict and disagreement.

- There was real clarity of focus.

- There were clear deadlines and guidelines.

- Things were predictable and orderly.

- _____
- _____
- _____

Phase III: Group and Categorize into Themes

Now that you have generated a list of things you have done that were particularly enjoyable or situations that made it so, review the list and group them into any similar patterns you might see. For example, you might group "You won awards," with "You were recognized for your contribution." You are simply looking for groupings that feel the same or similar to you. There is no right or wrong way to group them, but as with the vision exercise, less than three groups is too few, and more than 10 is likely too many.

In each of these groups, circle the words that resonate most with you. In the above example, you may feel that "recognized" resonates most or that both "awards" and "contribution" feel strongest.

Now, for each grouping, write a sentence that captures the conditions for when you are at your best. For example: *"I am at my best when I am recognized for my contributions and have the opportunity to win awards."*

When complete, you will have between three and 10 sentences that describe those conditions where you are at your best. These are your *unique themes of strengths, talents, and abilities.*

Example Results

The following page shows my own results for the first two phases of this exercise.

Phase I: Identify the Work You Have Enjoyed

- Technical Training Developer
- Documentation Manager
- Consultant
- Consulting Manager
- Associate Director
- Board President
- Commissioner
- President

Phase II: Identify Exactly What You Were Doing
Strategic Thinking

- I was able to solve problems and find solutions.
- I was able to sort through chaos and find the best path.
- I was allowed to brainstorm and come up with new ideas.
- I was allowed to figure out the best way to get things done.
- I was involved in **strategic discussions**.
- I was the visionary.

Taking Action

- I made things happen.
- **I took action.**
- I was given the authority to act on my judgment.
- I was in charge.

Create Maximum Results

- Goals were clearly defined and the tasks well understood.
- I was able to challenge others to get the best from themselves.
- I was not forced to settle for less than a **great output**.
- People really cared about performing at a high level.

Love of Learning

- I was able to **learn** a lot.
- I was allowed to brainstorm and come up with new ideas.
- I was challenged.

Connecting People and Ideas

- I was able to build meaningful relationships.
- I was communicating.
- I was or felt **connected** to everyone involved.

From the example, you can see the jobs and work that I enjoyed and the reasons why I enjoyed them. The example also shows these items grouped under the word or words that most resonate with me (in **bold**).

This then leads to the following definitions of my unique themes of strengths, talents and abilities.

- **Strategic Thinking:** I have the ability to sort through clutter and chaos to find the best route.

- **To Take Action:** I get things started and make things happen. I believe action speaks louder than words and that over analysis leads to paralysis!

- **Create Maximum Results:** I maximize other's personal strengths with excellence as the measure. If a task is worth doing, it is worth doing well. If I decide to do something, I do it with maximum effort.

- **Love of Learning:** I love learning, the process of discovery, and continually seek new knowledge and skills, especially when I need information to move me toward my vision and to support my personal mission and other themes of strength.

- **Connecting People and Ideas:** I believe that things happen for a reason because we are all connected. I am able to see connection between seemingly disparate ideas. This talent theme not only supports my strategic thinking talent theme, but also aides me in developing relationships with and between others.

More on Strengths

To help our clients discover their natural talents and strengths we have incorporated the Clifton StrengthsFinder®[7] test into our practice, an excellent tool provided by Gallup, Inc. To take the test, you must purchase a new copy of the book *Strengths Finder 2.0*, by Tom Rath, or *Strengths Based Leadership*, by Tom Rath and Barrie Conchie, both from Gallup Press. These books are available at your local bookstore or online bookseller and cost less than $30. If you would like to explore more deeply your strengths, we recommend that you purchase a new edition of one or both books. The value provided is priceless. A special one-time code is included in each book which allows you to take the online test(s). It will take about 30 minutes to read the first section of the book before it prompts you to take the test online. The test will take approximately 30 minutes to complete. The results will be yours – specific to you. Reading through the results and the listed talents in either book will be highly insightful and will help you better understand and confirm what you may have already gathered about yourself and your strengths from the exercises above. You may even have to admit that your Mom was right when she told you were good at... *you fill in the blank*!

---

7 The Clifton StrengthsFinder is a registered trademark of Gallup, Inc.

Evaluating Your Themes

Now that you have discovered your unique themes of strengths, talents, and abilities, let's take some time to figure out what all of this means. In general, this information is useful to determine and understand the following about yourself:

- Why you have enjoyed certain types of work or activities over others.

- Why certain work or tasks feel "easy," even without training, and others feel difficult, even with training.

- Why what you think is "easy" may be difficult for someone else and why what is "easy" for you is what makes you valuable.

- What your strengths can be, if developed through the acquisition of knowledge and skill.

- If properly developed and utilized, these strengths can lead to a personally fulfilling and meaningful career, one that is in true alignment with who you are.

- Your unique purpose in life, if it is not already clear to you, is most likely aligned with your strengths, or abilities, not your weaknesses or inabilities. If it is not already clear to you, your purpose is found by developing a deeper understanding of your strengths and by exploring vocations (careers) or avocations (hobbies) that requires these strengths for success and mastery. Now that you have some guidance, understanding, and direction about your strengths, you have a solid path on which to travel that will eventually lead you to your true purpose and personal fulfillment, even if it is not clear to you today.

- These strengths, when used to the extreme, also likely define your weaknesses or how people may see you in a negative sense. That is, our greatest strengths, *when taken to extreme*, become our greatest weaknesses. We will explore this concept in greater detail beginning on page 134.

For now, let's explore your list of themes a little more closely by asking yourself the following questions:

- When you read through the descriptions of your themes do you feel they describe you well or not? If not, you likely tried to describe who you WANT to be, rather than who you are today. Go back through the exercise and really focus on what is true now, not what you want to be true later.

- When you review the themes and the list of jobs you enjoyed, what types of careers or professions are indicated? This is the type of work you would likely enjoy and excel at in the future.

- You likely have had a desire to do - or to be - something nearly all your life. Look at that desire against these themes. How do the strengths needed for that career or activity and your themes correlate?

- Looking at the lists of jobs and activities you have compiled above, allow yourself to day dream a bit now. Which activities in the list really excite you, cause a curious spark, or give you that feeling of *"YES, that's what I have always wanted to do!"*?

- Take those thoughts a step further. What kind of training and/or education is required to enable you to do the career(s) or activities you outlined above? Does obtaining this type of training and education excite you? Do you have that training and education now? Pay attention to your energy during this process. If something revs you up and gets you going – it's likely in alignment with your strengths. If you begin to feel tense, suppressed, breathing a heavy sigh, and hanging your head – it's likely not the right fit for you.

The result of this analysis should give you a short list of two to three potential careers or hobbies that you have a *strong, positive feeling* about, and a desire to achieve. If you have a list greater than that, keep working through it until you get down to only two or three that really make you feel excited and energized.

It is important to note that it's OK to also feel fear or become worried about "how" you will make this all happen. "Becoming" the person you want to be, or learning a new career or skill can feel like a daunting task. This may even feel foreign to you if you have never allowed yourself to actually consider such possibilities before; it may even feel a bit silly. It's all OK! It's normal.

So trust the process so far. Don't try to rationalize too much. We'll do that later. Right now, we are still dreaming and envisioning...

On the other hand, you may be having a little trouble coming up with your "short list" or even anything that makes you feel really excited. No worries... that's OK too. There are still a few more factors to consider. If you are having difficulty getting to a short list, go back through the questions above once more and simply write down the first things that come to you and trust they will lead you to the right answers.

Also, understand - this IS a process. That is, even once you finish this book you may still be searching for THE career for you, or your true purpose, but you will have identified the options and possibilities most in alignment with your authentic self and eliminated those that are not, thereby saving you valuable time and effort. Remember, this is about the journey of "becoming," not about the destination, regardless of your age. No matter how old you are, you are valuable and you still have much more to *become.*

As a reminder of where this is leading us, your talents must be discovered and intentionally developed into strengths. Strengths must be intentionally developed by purposely acquiring knowledge with dedicated time spent practicing the appropriate skills. Sure, you CAN acquire knowledge and learn skills in anything you choose to do and feel good about it. Knowledge and skills are required for excellence. True personal fulfillment, however, comes when you develop your knowledge and skills from your inherent talents that are in alignment with your true self.

When you have created your short list of those professions, careers, or activities whereby the intentional acquisition of knowledge and dedicated practice of skill will put you in alignment with your true self, you will most likely feel excitement and find true personal fulfillment. That is, you will have begun to answer the question, *"Why am I here?"*

Strengths vs. Weaknesses

In our practice, by helping people discover their strengths, we have also discovered that, in most cases, we help people discover their weaknesses, or at least the ones others perceive in them. It goes something like this... An individual may discover that one of their strengths is the ability to command and control any situation. They can step in, take charge, and get results! What a great strength! Unfortunately, when this talent is taken to extreme, others may see them as pushy, bossy, and controlling, thus creating a "perceived weakness" that is actually one's strength, taken to extreme. Another individual discovers their strength is relating well with others. They can truly consider everyone's opinions and will work to ensure everyone's opinion is voiced and heard. Also a great strength! This person's "perceived weakness," however, may be that others view them as not having a mind of their own or incapable of independent thought or action. The net result of a lifetime of feedback from others (...that we need to "change" or stop behaving this way...) may result in us devaluing or even rejecting our unique strengths, believing they are a weakness.

In our society, many parents and educators stress the need to shore up one's weaknesses in order to succeed. We are literally taught to focus on those things we're not very good at doing, and pushed to work hard to overcome them in order to be "well rounded" and successful. Some believe it is a weak individual, weak of heart and mind who shies away from their weaknesses rather than digging in and working hard to diligently improve or overcome them. This is simply and utterly misguided!

In a few cases it is true that we must work to improve some weaknesses in order to be successful. This is true in educational endeavors and in many sports or professions. For example, if you have a weak jump shot in basketball, improving it may be needed for success, that is, IF you want to be a shooting guard. There are many great basketball players who have very weak jump shots. But they have other strengths, such as a nose for the ball, great passing ability, rebounding skills, and height. These great basketball players focused on their strengths, not their weaknesses, to get them where they are – playing at a professional level. You might be a business manager weak in mathematics. In order to be competent, you will at least need to bring your weakness up to an adequate level in the context of business math. But you would not have to make mathematics a strength and learn to solve differential equations in your sleep to be a successful business manager! We all have such "true inabilities." Things we are just not good at doing, or which take significant effort to accomplish. These things we need to either delegate to those who are gifted in that area or, more realistically, just let them go.

The real truth in all of this is, for most of us, focusing on our strengths is far more important, empowering, and much easier than a labored, grueling and drawn out focus on our weaknesses.

Some truths about strengths and weaknesses are:

- It takes far more effort to take a weakness to average ability than to take a strength to mastery. And we have already mentioned and will learn in greater detail shortly, we all desire and are motivated by mastery. It makes us feel good when we're *good* at something.

- Your weaknesses, regardless of how much you work on them, will never become true strengths. Yes, the rare few can, with extraordinary effort, turn a weakness around, but for most of us, our weaknesses will always be our weaknesses, requiring continuous extra effort to maintain an average outcome.

- You will use and count on your strengths each and every day. Strengths are the underlying engine for your life and career. They give you the tools for potential mastery and make the day-to-day enjoyable. When you are in alignment with your strengths the likelihood you will attain personal mastery of your craft and find personal fulfillment in your effort increases significantly.

- Conversely, a focus on your weaknesses may give you a life of constant trial and tribulation, forever pushing the rock up hill. It is time to let that go and put your focus on your strengths!

- As mentioned, often times the weaknesses others perceive in us are our strengths taken to extreme. While analyzing your strengths, look at how others might perceive them as negative, if taken to extreme. It is these "perceived weaknesses" that are often some of the most important "weaknesses" we have to overcome. That is, the negative perception of you by others is the "weakness" they see in you and think you need to "fix." Actually, all that really needs to be "fixed" is for you to learn to moderate your strength appropriately. Doing so is still a focus on, and a celebration of, your strengths. So for most of us, even a focus on what others see as a weakness in us is actually a focus on our strengths.

As an example, someone whose "strength theme" is focused on *activating* (i.e., getting things going and taking action), is always looking to get things started. To others, if the person with this strength acts this out to extreme, such behavior can be seen as undisciplined and impatient. Rather than "change" their strength and stop taking action, this person needs to use that strength appropriately and not rush to action without first considering the plan or the impact on others due to their quick action(s).

True Weaknesses

In our experience, we believe that weaknesses can be broken down into three categories, as shown in the following diagram:

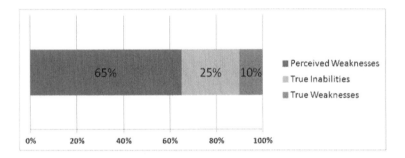

- **Perceived Weaknesses:** When we take our strengths to extreme we (through negative external or internal feedback) and others perceive this behavior as a *weakness*. In our work with clients, these generally constitute about 60-75% of the weaknesses people self-identify.

- **True Inabilities:** These are the things we are just not very good at. We do not have an innate ability or strength for these things and probably never will.

They are the things we may work hard to become adequate at doing, but will probably never master, no matter how hard we try. Here, our clients say that about 25-30% of their self-identified weaknesses are actually true inabilities. These can be "managed" simply by letting them go, delegating them to those who have the strength to master them, or live with the toil and angst required to complete them. We strongly suggest either of the former!

- **True weaknesses:** The true and only relevant weaknesses we see in people are ones of thought, attitude and belief, not aptitude. Thought, attitude and belief are weaknesses of *choice*. Some people choose a negative approach to life rather than a positive one. They choose to put themselves down rather than build themselves up. They choose not to believe in themselves and choose to believe something that impedes their life instead. They choose not to define and live a life of purpose, direction and integrity, or they simply chose to do nothing at all. For most of our clients, this equates to only 5-10% of their identified weaknesses, but this small percentage ends up being the most limiting, as you will see below.

Let's get any focus on weakness out of the way once and for all. Take a moment to list what you think your weaknesses are. Go ahead… get a piece of paper and a pencil and write them down, every one of them. Now, read them back to yourself. How do they make you feel?

Likely, pretty icky! No worries, we're going to turn them around right now. Read through your list again and consider the following:

- Was it a long or short list? What does a long list of weaknesses tell you about how you think of yourself? Do these thoughts indicate a positive approach to you and your life?

- Now, more closely examine the list. There will be three types of weaknesses; those which could be considered as taking one of your strengths to extreme, those that are a true inability, and those associated with a thought, belief or attitude about something. Try to identify which are which, and put them in three separate columns.

- For those focused on a strength taken to extreme, what could you do to change that extreme behavior? Are they truly weaknesses or simply strengths not used in the right context or in the best way? Would that behavior be considered extremely positive in a different work situation or social environment? In other words, is it you, or is it your choice of where and how you exercise that strength?

- For those listed as true inabilities, it is time to make a decision to either live with them, let them go, or delegate them to someone for whom this is a strength. Those are your only choices, unless, of course, you still believe it is best to toil away, day after day, forever pushing the rock uphill. It is more empowering and positive, however, to choose to let these things go or, if they are important to your life or business, to delegate them to someone who excels in that area.

- For those you listed in the column that are thought, attitude or belief-oriented, do these concern yourself, others, or the world or universe? Label each weakness to indicate whether it is about you, about others, or about the world in general. By the way, those are your only choices. Negative beliefs can only be about you, others, or the world in general.

- Now, for each of these negative beliefs, write the inverse positive statement. For example, if your stated weakness is, "*I am too heavy*," the inverse positive is, "*I am slim and fit*." If the stated weakness is, "*People just don't understand me*," the inverse positive would be, "*People understand me clearly*." If it is, "*The world is cold and unfair*," the inverse positive would be, "*The world is warm, friendly, and fair*."

Beginning on page 265 we will take these perceived "weaknesses" and create their inverse positive statements and build positive affirmations that will help you, once and for all, change any negative thoughts, beliefs and attitudes to create and encourage positive direction in your life.

The Bottom Line on Strengths vs. Weaknesses

The bottom line about strengths and weaknesses is this: A focus on weaknesses is a focus on the negative that drains your energy and diminishes you in the eyes of yourself, those around you, and the universe. *Only a positive focus on your strengths is an endeavor worthy of your time, effort, and energy.* It is empowering and uplifting and compels you forward toward the life of your dreams and all that you desire! Perceived weaknesses can be managed and, ultimately, nearly eliminated by a focus on your strengths. True inabilities can be accepted and let go, eliminating them from consideration. True weaknesses can, because they are one-hundred percent controlled by you and your thoughts, attitudes and beliefs, be turned into their "counter-positive" belief.

The Personal Profile is the tool in which you will describe your unique themes of strength, talent and ability and how you can use them in a positive way to move your life forward. You will also explore and describe your "perceived weaknesses" and how to manage them to reduce their potential negative impact on your life. This exploration is an important fundamental building block in your journey of a life based on a continual, positive focus on your strengths. This is the power and confidence that you receive when you *Live from Strength*.

Learning Styles

"The single biggest problem in communication is the illusion that it has taken place."
George Bernard Shaw

"To effectively communicate, we must realize that we are all different in the way we perceive the world and use this understanding as a guide to our communication with others."
Anthony Robins

Remember in school when some of your classes seemed easy and fun while others were tedious, boring, and difficult? Or perhaps you had a supervisor at work who you seemed to get along with well and communication was easy and clear, while others seemed to struggle to get their point across and were difficult to "figure out" or understand. If you are the boss or a supervisor, does some of your staff "get you" while others don't? Do some of your daily tasks - such as information processing, creating reports or reading graphs, building shelves, paying bills, etc. - seem easy while others seem to be, literally, a dreaded chore (making cold calls, public speaking, group presentations, talking with customer service to resolve a problem)? From a family perspective, if you have more than one child or sibling, do you seem to communicate better with one than the other, or do you enjoy being around one sibling more than another?

Take a few moments to think about those times where taking in or using information just seemed easy. Is there a common theme to how the information was being presented? Was it visual with pictures or graphs? Did you read it or hear it? Did you get to practice it, touch it, or manipulate it? It is highly likely in those cases the information was presented to you in a way that aligns with your inherent learning and information processing style.

There are numerous theories regarding learning styles, from the basic "learning modality" theory [visual (see), auditory (hear) and kinesthetic (do)] which we use in our practice, to the more complex theories outlined by authors such as Dr. Howard Gardner[8] who proposes up to eight separate "intelligences":

- verbal/linguistic
- logical/mathematical
- visual/spatial
- bodily/kinesthetic
- musical
- interpersonal

---

8 Multiple Intelligences, Howard Gardner, Basic Books, 2006.

Live from Strength

- intrapersonal

- naturalistic

There are also those theories that form the basis for most "personality tests," such as the Myers-Briggs Type Indicator[9] (extroversion/introversion, sensing/intuition, thinking/feeling, judgment/perception).

For the purposes of discovering and developing your unique gifts, let's keep it simple and look at the *basic* learning styles a little more closely:

- *Auditory:* Learning and processing occurs primarily though hearing the spoken word. This includes reading, which for most people is more like *hearing* the words in their head as they read. Auditory learners may often say, "*I hear you,*" when they have received a message effectively, regardless of how it was delivered, or may say something like, "*say that again,*" or "*tell me again,*" when they need more information.

- *Visual:* Learning and processing occurs primarily through viewing images, demonstrations, body language and creating mind-maps. Visual learners may often say, "*I see that*" when they have received a message effectively, regardless of how it was delivered, or may say something like, "*let me see that again,*" or "*show me again,*" when they need more information.

---

9 Myers, Isabel Briggs with Peter B. Myers (1980, 1995). Gifts Differing: Understanding Personality Type. Mountain View, CA: Davies-Black Publishing

- *Tactile/Kinesthetic:* Learning and processing occurs primarily through doing and interacting, touching, and feeling. Kinesthetic learners may often say, *"I feel it,"* or *"I get you,"* or *"I feel the same"* when they have received a message effectively, regardless of how it was delivered, or may say something like, *"give me that again,"* or *"let me do that again,"* when they need more information.

Beginning on page 152, we provide an assessment to help you determine whether you are dominant in one style or have some combination of learning styles.

Regardless of the learning style theories identified here, your unique combination of learning styles has the following impacts on you and your personal growth, as well as your Personal Mission Statement:

- Most of us have a dominant, natural learning style - or way of processing incoming information. Thus, knowing and understanding your natural style will help you to ask your family, friends, supervisors and/or staff for, and receive information in the way that works best for you. Imagine the impact on your productivity in your job if all information coming your way was easily understood with clear directions allowing you to act on it right away. Imagine the impact this might have in your personal relationships too!

- You likely communicate with others in the style that is best for you and you may find it difficult to communicate in other ways. You may not have even considered that there was any other way to communicate as "my way" just seems to make sense – to you. But as a communicator, *it is your job* to relay information, assign tasks, and communicate to those you love and work with in a clear and effective manner. If communicating is the responsibility of the communicator, then learning how to communicate in a variety of methods is THE essential communication skill.

- People generally find work or avocations more enjoyable when they are in alignment with their natural learning style. Those that are visual learners might enjoy work in the visual arts or find conceiving graphics for presentations to be fun and easy. The graphic design and architecture industries tend to "speak" visually with videos and elaborate presentations. Those who are auditory may become great linguists, speakers, or writers, and those in the industry will tend to tell stories to communicate. Those who are kinesthetic may enjoy physical work and working with their hands (such as construction work, an auto mechanic, or a barista) or can't wait to get home to tend to the garden or work in the garage. As a business owner or manager in the workplace, the more you can align someone to positions and tasks that are in alignment with their learning styles, the more happy and productive they will be. Most importantly, the more you can align yourself to professions that speak and communicate like you do, the happier you will be in your work.

- There is no one "best way" of presenting information, there is only the way that is best for the individual receiving it. As a communicator, therefore, we should know and understand the needs of those to whom we are communicating, and if we can't know ahead of time (such as in a large group presentation) then it is important to use many different modalities in your presentation. For example, always have a visual, coupled with printed materials, and provide a way for the tactile learner to "touch and feel" the information, even if that is simply providing a place on a hand-out to take notes as you speak. Be active and animated, pointing and referring to your visuals. Involve the crowd by asking questions, have them speak to their neighbor, discuss ideas in small groups, or complete a tactile task on their own or as a team.

- Many people, perhaps even the majority, have some level of difficulty in processing information in one form or another. A rare few, perhaps 10% of the population, can learn equally well in any modality and an equally rare few have specific, definable learning disabilities. The rest of us figure out a way to learn and process information effectively with the learning style(s) we possess. This means that in life (work, friends and family), most of the people you come in contact with will have some difficultly processing information in one or more ways, yet they can still be highly successful if they get the information in the way they process best.

- Some psychologists believe each modality or intelligence can be developed or improved. In our practice, we have helped people learn to use tools to more effectively process and communicate information. There is no research or techniques that we have found, however, that suggests people can ever change their dominant learning styles. With regard to living from strength, this means we must focus on the positive aspects of our own learning style as a means to achieve personal success while considering the learning styles of others to improve our personal communication.

- It is important to focus on people's strengths. It is not necessary to identify people's weaknesses or try to "fix" them. Though you may perceive it a weakness that someone can't "get you" when you show them something, grabbing someone's mouse and quickly clicking around the screen to demonstrate a process will only leave you and the tactical learner frustrated when you have to explain it to them again. Even though you may be able to watch (see) someone else do something and remember it, others must experience and manually go through each step themselves before they can remember the process. No matter how often someone blurts out directions, often at ever increasing volumes, and then walks away, the visual learner still won't get it! Providing some form of visual, however, to accompany the directions will likely help. Can't draw? No problem, have the visual learner draw it for you as they try to explain the meaning of what they just heard. Having a positive and tolerant approach will lead to a much more productive and happy work force and family life. Remember, it isn't the receiver of the information who needs to change, it's how the communicator delivers the information in order to be understood.

- Differences in processing information in a given modality or having a learning disability, is not the same as a lack of intelligence. Many individuals living with a learning disability are highly intelligent and high functioning, stuck behind the "disabled" label. We believe learning disabled people are usually highly capable once information is presented to them in the way that THEY learn best and tools are provided to them so - like the rest of us - they can work around their difficulty. The blunt impact of this knowledge is that as communicators, we need to re-evaluate any thoughts we may have about how "smart" someone is and begin thinking more about how smart WE are in our own ability to communicate with everyone.

By understanding how we best learn and process information and by understanding that everyone, regardless of intelligence, likely processes information differently than we do, we can begin to create a more productive and harmonious life for ourselves and those around us. We can let people know how best to present ideas and information to us. We can present information in a variety of modalities to reach more people. We can be patient with those who "just don't get it" and begin to understand that they likely don't understand because we have not communicated in the way they CAN "get it." And we can give our workforce and our families the tools, knowledge, and understanding about the impacts of learning styles on effective communication and help those around us become better, more effective communicators.

And for yourself, choosing to work in a career and profession that better aligns with your method of information processing is one of the most important things you will discover from understanding your own learning style. Doing so will lead you to a happier and more fulfilling life and career, and allow you to *Live from Strength*!

Now, it is time to determine your learning style so you can apply this knowledge while developing your Personal Mission Statement.

The Learning Style Assessment

Take a few minutes to complete the following questionnaire to assess your *general* or basic preferred learning style (visual, auditory, or kinesthetic). Begin by reading the words in the left-hand column. Of the three responses to the right, circle the one that best characterizes you, answering as honestly as possible with the description that applies to you *right now*. Count the number of circled items and write your total at the bottom of each column. Following the questionnaire, we provide additional questions to help you better understand and analyze the results. The answers will offer insight into how you learn.

1. When I try to concentrate...	I grow distracted by clutter or movement, and I notice things around me other people don't notice.	I get distracted by sounds, and I attempt to control the amount and type of noise around me.	I become distracted by commotion, and I tend to retreat inside myself.
2. When I visualize...	I see vivid, detailed pictures in my thoughts.	I think in voices and sounds.	I see images in my thoughts that involve movement.
3. When I talk with others...	I find it difficult to listen for very long.	I enjoy listening, or I get impatient to talk myself.	I gesture and "talk" with my hands.

4. When I contact people...	I prefer face-to-face meetings.	I prefer speaking by telephone for serious conversations.	I prefer to interact while walking or participating in some activity.
5. When I see someone I have met...	I forget names but remember faces, and I tend to replay where we met for the first time.	I know people's names and I can usually quote what we discussed.	I remember what we did together and I may almost "feel" our time together.
6. When I relax...	I watch TV, see a play, visit an exhibit, or go to a movie.	I listen to the radio, play music, read, or talk with a friend.	I play sports, make crafts, or build something with my hands.
7. When I read...	I like descriptive examples and I may pause to imagine the scene.	I enjoy the narrative most and I can almost "hear" the characters talk.	I prefer action-oriented stories, but I do not often read for pleasure.
8. When I spell...	I envision the word in my mind or imagine what the word looks like when written.	I sound out the word, sometimes aloud, and tend to recall rules about letter order.	I get a feel for the word by writing it out or pretending to type it.
9. When I do something new...	I seek out demos, pictures or diagrams.	I want verbal and written instructions, and to talk it over with someone else.	I jump right in to try it, keep trying, and try different approaches.
10. When I assemble an object...	I look at the picture first and then, maybe, read the directions.	I read the directions, or I talk aloud as I work.	I usually ignore the directions and figure it out as I go along.

Learning Styles   153

11. When I interpret someone's mood...	I examine facial expressions.	I rely on listening to tone of voice.	I focus on body language.
12. When I teach other people...	I draw them a picture or diagram.	I tell them, write it out, or I ask them a series of questions.	I show how it is done and then ask them to try.
Total	Visual:	Auditory Verbal:	Tactile/ Kinesthetic:

Understanding Your Learning Style Results

Once you have completed the Learning Styles Assessment, answer the following questions to better understand the results:

- Is there a column with clearly a larger number of answers selected? Did you find that you easily answered the questions in that column over the others? If you have a column that has a significantly greater number than the other two, then you likely have a very dominant learning style. That is, you likely need to learn and communicate in that method and find it difficult to learn in others.

- Are there two columns with relatively the same number of answers and one column with relatively few? Did you find yourself vacillating between choosing the statements in those two columns? If you have two relatively even columns and one with very few answers, then you likely can learn effectively in either method, but most likely need to experience both to learn most effectively.

- Do you have relatively even answers across all columns? If you do and found it difficult to choose between the three columns because all the answers seemed to relate to you, then you might be one of the truly gifted learners who can learn in any modality. Once again, however, the flip side is that you may require all modalities to learn most effectively, which can be difficult to achieve in all learning situations.

- Did you find it hard to select one answer in each column because NO answer seemed to best describe you? If you had no dominant number in any one column and found it difficult to choose because none of the answers seemed to fit, you may be one of the few who needs further testing because the test provided here is too general. If so, you may need a more detailed or clinical analysis from a certified learning specialist. You also, as above, may be able to learn in all modalities; however, you will likely need to use past and future experience to truly determine if you have a dominant style or if you can learn in all modalities.

Do the results align with your experience? When you think back, what classes in school did you excel in? Did you tend to do well in classes where the teacher presented information in the dominant method suggested by this assessment? What about the classes or teachers you didn't understand? How was the information in those classes presented? Now think about a work situation. Did you have a boss you "clicked with," or you easily understood and rarely needed additional clarification to perform a task? How did they communicate with you and was their communication style in alignment with the results of your assessment? How about bosses you did not communicate well with? How did they communicate with you? Now think about a family situation. Is there a family member you love but can't be around very long because you can't talk to him? Or do you have one child you seem to understand better than another?

Now, consider how *you* think and communicate. Those who are visual learners tend to think in pictures or want to grab a pen and a piece of paper and draw pictures or graphs to explain themselves. They use words and expressions such as, "*see what I mean?*" Auditory learners have a very strong vocabulary and use very expressive words when they talk. They constantly look for the word that best describes the situation and desire precision in their speech. They ask "*do you hear me?*" or "*do you understand me?*" Tactical/Kinesthetic learners tend to communicate by showing or demonstrating, and often do so without many explanatory words. They ask if you are "*with them*" or if you "*feel*" that you understand.

How does your experience then, in terms of both how you have learned in the past and how you tend to communicate, align with your assessment results? If they align fairly well, then you now know your dominant learning style and/or that you can learn fairly well in multiple styles. If on the other hand, you are the rare exception and this assessment did not provide clarity, then the only question is whether you have, in the past, found learning and communicating fairly easy or extremely difficult. If easy, then it is likely you have the ability to use all the modalities and you have no dominant style. This is a good thing and should be celebrated!

If, on the other hand, the test did not provide a clear answer and you have had difficulty learning or communicating in the past, you may find it valuable to see a certified learning specialist to discover techniques and ways to help you learn and communicate more effectively. Almost everyone can learn and communicate better, and a few will need professional assistance from a learning specialist to find the right combination of techniques to do so most effectively.

As with your strengths, you will describe and define your unique learning and communication style, and what the assessment above means to your life, in your Personal Profile. You will also describe how to best use your natural learning style to *Live from Strength™* while understanding how to consider the other learning styles to improve your communication.

Motivation: An Inside Job

"Your distress about life might mean you have been living for the wrong reason, not that you have no reason for living."
Tom O'Conner

A lot of time and energy has been used conducting studies on how to motivate people at work or around the house when the real question is how are people "naturally" motivated? What internal "hot buttons" get you up, get you going, and provide the energy to sustain you through to completion of a task?

The real questions to answer as you build your Personal Strategic Foundation are - how are YOU *naturally* and *normally* motivated, and how does that natural, or intrinsic style impact your feeling of fulfillment and purpose in your career or profession and in your personal life? That is, how are you naturally inspired to take action?

What You Need To Know About Motivation

There is considerable research and many theories about motivation. Some of this research centers on the question of *why* we act, and others are focused on *how* we can motivate others to do something, particularly in the work environment or in the home environment as we raise our children. Most of this research ends up providing us with the following conclusions:

- That we, as humans, act to fulfill a need and when needs are satisfied we are no longer compelled to act. Abraham Maslow's *Hierarchy of Human Needs* theory[10] is the most prominent and widely discussed theory regarding motivation. The foundation of his theory states that all people have basic needs such as food and shelter, and higher order needs such as love, self esteem, and self actualization. We act to fulfill the basic needs first and once those are met, the higher order needs can be pursued.

- In the workplace, one can either be positively compelled to act by certain external or extrinsic factors, called *motivators*, or de-motivated by the absence or inadequate levels of other factors, called *hygiene factors*. Frederick Herzberg's "Motivator-Hygiene" theory[11]

10 Motivation and Personality (1st Edition: 1954, 2nd Edition: 1970, 3rd Edition 1987), Abraham Maslow, Robert Frager and James Fadiman.
11 The Motivation to Work, New York: John Wiley and Sons, 1959, 'One more time: How do you motivate employees?', Harvard Business Review, Sep/Oct87, Vol. 65 Issue 5, p109-120

states that when the positive motivators are present and people are satisfied with the hygiene factors (such as good company policies, positive supervision, functioning computers, appropriate salary, strong interpersonal relations on the job, and healthy working conditions), the most positive motivational conditions exist in the workplace. When the hygiene factors are not "healthy" (such as unclear company policies, negative supervision, problematic computer functions, inappropriate salary levels, poor interpersonal relations on the job, and unhealthy working conditions), people's motivation or mental health deteriorates (which explains why the term "hygiene" is used to describe these factors, as the mental "cleanliness" or hygiene of business deteriorates) and people become "de-motivated."

- There are two types of motivators, *intrinsic* (from within) and *extrinsic* (from outside yourself).

- Extrinsic motivators can work to cause one to take action, but are not sustaining if the individual's intrinsic motivations are not in alignment with the situation.

- Negative motivators, such as fear, can work for a short time but have tremendous negative impacts on the relationships involved.

- Most all extrinsic motivators that work are centered on personal growth and fulfillment, or professional growth and fulfillment, or the higher levels of Maslow's Hierarchy of Human Needs, rather than on materialistic rewards such as money (that is, money is RARELY a long-term personal motivator).

- Long-term and sustaining performance occurs only when you are intrinsically motivated and when external factors do not suppress that internal drive. Motivation, when all is said and done, is really an "inside job." You must motivate yourself. Someone else cannot do it for you. Yes, you can be "inspired" by others, but personal motivation comes from within.

- Our intrinsic motivators can be categorized in two major groups; those intrinsic motivators that apply to all of us, and those that are unique to you.

- As we will describe in more detail in the next section, Daniel Pink in his book *Drive,* examined much of this information to conclude that *all of us* are motivated by a desire for *mastery, purpose* and *autonomy.* That is, each of us seeks these outcomes in our life. Thus, all of us will naturally act to create these situations in our life, and tend not to act on things when these desires are not met.

- You are *uniquely* motivated to act, according to David McClelland,[12] a noted American psychologist, by one of three main needs-based intrinsic motivators: a dominant need for *achievement*; a dominant need for *affiliation*; and a dominant need for *power*.

- In order to develop your Personal Strategic Foundation, you need to determine how you are *uniquely intrinsically* motivated so you can learn to cultivate it, and then find or create situations where the best external conditions exist so that all your intrinsic motivations can be released most effectively.

Using This Information About Motivation

It is critical to understand *how* you are naturally motivated so you can make choices to align yourself with a career, profession, or life choice (such as becoming a CEO for a mid-sized company, or a stay-at-home parent) that is most suited to you. This life choice will already have an environment that inspires you to be naturally motivated. Knowing how you are naturally motivated also keeps you from going into situations and environments where you will be asked to do things that could actually de-motivate you.

---

12 David C. McClelland, "Methods of Measuring Human Motivation", in John W. Atkinson, ed., *The Achieving Society* (Princeton, N.J.: D. Van Nostrand, 1961), pp. 41-43.

Another important aspect of this knowledge is to understand that once you are in alignment with your natural motivations, only then can you assess your creativity, competence, and passion. Have you ever said to yourself in the past, "*I'm not very creative,*" or, "*I'm not very competent*" when it comes to a certain area of your life? Most of us have at some point in our lives, or you may find yourself there now! This likely means you have not yet had the opportunity to live or work in situations more in alignment with your natural motivators, strengths, and learning styles. But once you are in an environment more suited to *who* you are, it is like the light bulb goes on inside you and all of a sudden you become highly creative, you discover you are "gifted" in the competencies of this role, and you begin to feel true passion for what you are doing. You will experience moments where you think "*Wow, this is better than* _____!" (Well, you fill in the blank...)

When you are in alignment with your natural motivators you open yourself up to new opportunities that can create the ideal conditions for internal inspiration. Inspiration is the real driver of your life and career. When you feel inspired, you can literally move mountains to achieve your objectives. Inspiration springs from within. Inspiration comes from your true self.

Rather than look for outside influences to kick-start your personal motivation, the idea is to be in alignment with your natural motivators so true organic inspiration can occur. By understanding how you are naturally motivated and choosing to align yourself to that knowledge, you will find yourself, perhaps for the first time, naturally inspired. Ideas will flow, desire will well forth, and the confidence to take action will seemingly come from nowhere! In the end, motivation is an inside job and true motivation - the motivation to overcome and see things through - comes from a feeling of internal inspiration.

Dr. Phil McGraw[13] says it this way. "Motivation can wax and wane... When your willpower is nowhere to be found, you need to have your emotions, logic, environment, behavior, food plan, exercise, and social support system in place to keep you in the right direction." When you have organized your life so that external motivation, such as starting a new exercise program, is not the only thing you count on to move you forward, this is true alignment. In fact, your life is naturally moving you forward BECAUSE you are aligned.

Types of Intrinsic Motivators

Our intrinsic motivators can be categorized in two major groups; those intrinsic motivators that apply to all of us and those that are unique to you.

---

13 McGraw PhD, P.C., (2005) in Live Your Best Life; A Treasury of Wisdom, Wit, Advice, Interviews, and Inspiration from O, The Oprah Magazine, Birmingham, AL, Oxmoor House, p 13

Motivators That Apply to Us All

Based on Daniel Pink's research mentioned earlier, we are all motivated to act in three basic ways:

- *Autonomy*: This is the desire to be in charge of one's life, to make your own decisions.

- *Mastery*: This is the desire to be truly excellent at something. To master a skill, vocation or craft.

- *Purpose*: This is the desire for purpose and meaning in life, to be part of something larger than yourself.

As you can readily see, these intrinsic motivators align perfectly with many of the aspects we describe in *"a life well lived,"* on page 32. It is no wonder then that personal fulfillment in life comes, in no small part, from personal mastery aligned to your unique gifts, working and living for a higher purpose aligned to your Personal Mission, and to being the master of your own destiny through the power of a compelling vision. Ah-ha!

Our Unique Motivators

Based on the work done by David McClelland mentioned earlier, there are three main needs-based intrinsic motivators for which each person has a **unique** style: a dominant need for *achievement*; a dominant need for *affiliation*; and a dominant need for *power*. McClelland's work, and that done by those who followed him, indicates that each of us is motivated in all three ways but to varying and unique degrees. Further, most of us have one dominant need while some have two rather equally dominant needs, and a rare few are relatively equally motivated in all three ways. Additionally, McClelland theorized that our unique mix of motivators (or dominant needs) were "hard-wired" in all of us by the age of 17. That is, nature and nurture has created in all of us a dominant need that drives our behavior on a consistent and daily basis throughout our lives.

Applying Your Unique Motivation

What does this mean to you and your Personal Strategic Foundation? The more you can find a profession or a particular job or lifestyle choice where the needs of that choice are in alignment with your unique intrinsic motivator(s) and supports your need for autonomy, mastery and purpose, the more successful and personally fulfilled you will likely be. More importantly, to truly find your passion in life and the answer to the question, *"Why am I here?"* you will likely find it in vocations and endeavors that are in alignment with your natural unique intrinsic motivators, learning styles, and strengths. This is why it is important to assess your motivators *before* building your Personal Mission Statement.

Let's look at the three types of unique intrinsic motivators in more detail:

- *Achievement:* People with a high need for achievement have a need to succeed and they seek to excel. They are motivated by setting and achieving objectives and winning and finishing at the top of their class. They have, and set, high standards for themselves. Because they seek to achieve, they also tend to avoid both low-risk and high-risk situations. Predominantly achievement-motivated individuals avoid low-risk situations because easily attained success is not a genuine achievement, at least in their minds. In high-risk situations, those who are achievement-motivated see the outcome as one of chance rather than one's own effort, and consequently avoid it. High achievement-motivated individuals prefer work and projects that have a moderate probability of success, ideally 50% or greater. That is, they are NOT risk takers. Careers where high achievement is correlated to success are business related; an entrepreneur, sales, real estate agent or owner-manager of a small business. Achievement-motivated individuals need regular feedback in order to monitor the progress of their achievements. They prefer either to work alone or with others like themselves.

- *Affiliation:* Those with a high need for affiliation need harmonious relationships with other people. They need to feel accepted and feel a sense of involvement and "belonging" within a social group. They tend to conform to the norms of their work group. High affiliation-motivated individuals prefer work that provides significant personal interaction, warm interpersonal relationships, and approval from those with whom they have regular contact. They tend to be supportive team and family members, but may be less effective in leadership positions because of their need to be liked. They enjoy being part of a group and make excellent team members, though sometimes are distractible into social interaction. They can perform well in customer service and client interaction situations.

- *Power:* A person's need for power can be one of two types - *personal* and *institutional.* Those who need personal power want to direct others, and this need often is perceived as undesirable when it is taken to extreme with the desire to have power OVER others. Persons who need institutional power (also known as social power) want to organize the efforts of others to further the goals of the organization or family. Managers with a high need for institutional power tend to be more effective than those with a high need for personal power. They are likely to be most satisfied by seeing their work or family environment move in a certain direction due to their influence, involvement and leadership.

Discovering Your Natural Unique Motivation

To complete this exercise, read the statement in the first column of the table below then read each of the statements in columns A through C that potentially completes the sentence. For each possible answer, rate your agreement with the complete statement on a scale of zero to 10. If you agree completely, rate it a 10. If you don't agree at all, rate it a zero. Rate all three statements; however, the total in all three columns must add up to 10. Read all three possible responses before rating each one.

Example: For the first statement you might place 7 in column A, indicating you agree strongly with it; 3 in column B, indicating you agree somewhat with it; and 0 in column C indicating you do not agree at all with that statement.

Any combination of agreement from 10-0-0 to 4-3-3 is acceptable; however, there will always be one column you are most in agreement with (4).

Statement	A	B	C
When I work in a group or team...	I feel frustrated with all the talk and just want to get it done myself. _____	I feel invigorated and really enjoy working together toward a common goal. _____	I like to be in a leadership role and I tend to take charge in meetings. _____
I find I do my best work when...	I have clear goals and objectives. _____	I can work with others and be part of a team. _____	I am in charge or in a position of authority. _____
I like to work best...	By myself. _____	With others. _____	Managing people or projects. _____
When I work by myself...	I feel in control and can best impact the outcome. _____	I feel less connected to the outcome. _____	I feel less able to affect the outcome. _____
When I am called on to be in charge...	I make sure there are clear goals and objectives. _____	I work to build consensus and buy-in from those I am leading. _____	I really take charge and lead the group. _____

Statement	A	B	C
The best manager I ever had...	Set clear goals and objectives and provided feedback on progress.	Included me in decisions and made me feel part of the team.	Gave me the project and let me lead.
What gets me up in the morning is...	The opportunity to get things done and tick items off my list.	Working with great people to achieve a common objective.	Being the person in charge and making things happen.
The best job I ever had...	I worked by myself and was rewarded for achieving goals.	I worked with others and enjoyed the camaraderie of my teammates.	I led a project or team that created real value for the company.
When I set goals for myself...	I almost always reach them.	I sometimes reach them, especially when I am accountable to the team.	I am the one who sets goals for others.
Getting the acceptance and appreciation of others is...	Nice, but really not that important.	What I live for.	Acceptance? I want respect!

SCORING: Add up the values in each column to determine your dominant intrinsic unique motivation style (the one with the largest value), and your secondary intrinsic motivation style.

TOTALS: _____ _____ _____

Dominant Unique Motivation Style: If the largest number is:

- Column A, you have a dominant need for *Achievement*.

- Column B, you have a dominant need for *Affiliation*.

- Column C, you have a dominant need for *Power*.

Secondary Unique Motivation Style: If the next largest number is:

- Column A, you have a secondary need for *Achievement*.

- Column B, you have a secondary need for *Affiliation*.

- Column C, you have a secondary need for *Power*.

Circle your dominant and secondary motivation styles above.

Note: Any combination of totals may be seen from highly dominant to relatively even and there are no "right" combinations. What IS important is whether the results appear to represent how you are truly motivated.

This exercise will give you a probable indication of your intrinsic motivation; however, there are more exacting tests that require a trained facilitator in the McClelland method to execute. If after assessing the results below you are still not certain what your personal motivators are, you may wish to find a trained facilitator in your area to conduct a more detailed assessment.

Confirming and Evaluating Results

Looking at your results from the previous exercises, answer the following questions:

- Think about past jobs or activities you really enjoyed where you felt good about what you did (refer to the strengths themes assessment on page 130). What kind of situation was it? Did it require motivation and action more aligned with power, affiliation, or achievement? Does that align with the dominant motivation styles from the completed exercise?

- Now think about previous jobs or activities you did not enjoy or where you did not feel satisfied by what you accomplished. What kind of motivation was required for that work? Does that align with your non-dominant motivation styles?

If you answered yes to both questions above, then you can be very confident with your results. Now, consider what these results tell you about the type of work that best suits your motivation style. Use your experience and your personal vision to assist you in answering the following questions:

- What type of activities would this work involve? For example, if you are motivated by "power," you might desire activities that require you to be in charge of others or be in charge of managing processes to create success. A person motivated by "affiliation" may desire to work as part of a team or work where their activities contribute to a cause or the success of the organization as a whole. For those motivated by "achievement," they might desire activities where they can work independently or where their individual efforts directly lead to results.

- What are the attributes of this work environment that will help you be your best? For example, if you are motivated by "power," you may desire a work environment that is process driven or where managing people and controlling processes are highly valued. As someone motivated by "affiliation," you may desire a team oriented work environment or to work for a non-profit because everyone is working toward a cause you believe in. "Achievement" motivated individuals may flourish in an environment where individual achievement is highly valued.

- What type of management style would best motivate you? For those motivated by "power," having clear objectives set by upper management and being given the authority to get things done may work best. For those motivated by "affiliation," they may perform best for managers who provide constant feedback and praise to their staff for a job well done. "Achievers," on the other hand, may work best with "hands off" managers who simply assigns them a task, sets the deadline, and provides the resources needed so they can get the job done.

Use the information above to create a description of the "ideal work" that fits your motivation style. This includes the type of activities, the type of work environment, and the type of management style that would allow your natural motivation to be released.

NOTE: If you answered "no" to either or both of the initial questions in this section, it does not necessarily mean the results were wrong. It may simply mean that you can be motivated by any of the three motivators, or that you were able to motivate yourself for a brief period to get the job done. If you are unsure of the results, you may want to contact a local facilitator who can conduct a McClelland method assessment.

At this point, you have done the homework. Now let's continue the journey by first compiling the information you have discovered about your unique gifts into a comprehensive Personal Profile that we will use as the basis for creating your first Personal Mission Statement!

Your Personal Profile

*Look well into thyself; there is a source of strength which
will always spring up if thou wilt always look there.*
Marcus Aurelius

*Always be a first-rate version of yourself,
instead of a second-rate version of somebody else.*
Judy Garland

If you want to discover your unique purpose so you can use it to create real value in this world and bring meaning and fulfillment to your life, and if the foundation of that unique purpose consists of your strengths, learning style, and natural way of being motivated, then putting this information into a comprehensive and detailed Personal Profile is a strong and powerful *first step* to defining your unique purpose; your Personal Mission Statement.

In addition, as we *imagined* earlier, imagine the POWER of truly knowing your unique gifts! This is the POWER, confidence, and freedom that come from knowing and having at hand, at any moment, the most effective way for you to manage any task, handle any situation while aligning your actions to your authentic self. This power can only come from knowing yourself. Thus, creating a clear and comprehensive Personal Profile is an indispensable tool for living from strength as it literally defines what those strengths and unique gifts are and how you can best utilize them in a positive way.

Your Personal Profile consists of the following:

- Your unique themes of talents and abilities.

- Your natural way of learning and communicating.

- Your natural way of being motivated.

You will go beyond simple lists and create detailed and comprehensive descriptions of your talents and unique abilities that not only define you, but resonate deep inside you as a true and accurate description and representation of your unique gifts. When you read them out loud, after you have defined them for yourself, you want the feeling within you to be *"YES! This is who I am! This is who I am truly meant to be!"*

In addition, for each unique capability, you will understand the implications these have on the type of work in which you would excel, feel aligned to, and would give you personal fulfillment. You will also understand how your unique strengths may impact relationships and personal interactions. Included in this process, you will understand how, when taken to extreme, your unique strengths may be perceived as a weakness in the eyes of others and you will describe how you will mitigate these potential negative impacts of your strengths taken to extreme.

Like many things in this process, creating a truly meaningful Personal Profile may be a challenge *at first*. As you move forward and reflect on your strengths and natural abilities, and as you practice using them intentionally in your life, you will gain greater understanding of their impact on the world around you. It is important to remember that your Personal Profile will grow and deepen as you do. It is a "work in progress," as you are. To begin, simply focus on getting the basics down on paper. As you review and revise your Personal Annual Action Plan you will have many opportunities to revise and update your Personal Profile as you become more aware of the POWER of living in alignment with your unique gifts.

Creating Your Personal Profile

Creating your Personal Profile begins by simply creating a document in which you include the results of the exercises completed over the last three chapters. If you are working electronically, create an electronic document entitled, "My Personal Profile." If you are not using a computer, take a piece of paper and write, "My Personal Profile" at the top.

Beginning with your unique themes of talents and abilities, list each one in this document. Using the results of the clarifying questions found on page 130, create a description of each "strength." If you used the StrengthsFinder®, you can review the description of each of your top five strengths, find the statements that resonate most with you, and place them in your document to create a description of how this strength is unique to you.

Next, list your natural learning and communication style. Refer back to the questions beginning on page 154 and create a description of what this learning style means to you.

Finally, list your dominant and secondary way of being motivated and refer to the questions beginning on page 174 to create a description of how this uniquely applies to you.

Example of a Personal Profile

Starting on the next page is my Personal Profile as one example of how this might look. Feel free to put your Personal Profile together, formatted in a way that makes sense for you. Those who are visual may choose to use pictures rather than just words for a Visual Personal Profile.

Wayne Ottum's Personal Profile

My Unique Strengths

I utilize the following personal strengths:

- **Strategic Thinking:** I have the ability to sort through clutter and chaos to find the best route. Because I see answers before others, I must be patient to allow others to see the answers themselves. This means that sometimes, I have to keep the answers I see to myself so as not to appear overly opinionated or arrogant to others.

- **To Take Action:** I get things started and make things happen. I believe action speaks louder than words and that over analysis leads to paralysis. Because I am ready for action before most people, I need to consciously focus on patience while helping others prepare for action in a way that works best for them.

- **Create Maximum Results:** I maximize other's personal strengths with excellence as the measure. If a task is worth doing, it is worth doing right. If I decide to do something, I do it with maximum effort. In order for this strength not to be perceived as a weakness to others, I need to be aware that my view of "maximum results" may not be the view of others and allow them to define the results they desire whenever the situation allows.

- **Love of Learning:** I love learning and continually seek new knowledge and skills, especially in alignment with my other themes of strength. My love of learning is not a love of "having knowledge" but of the process of discovery. I am not, therefore, a keeper of knowledge, trivia, or things that are not of immediate importance, but rather a keeper of the process of finding the information when I need it. Others may see this as a weakness in that I may seem disinterested when I do not see an immediate need for the information they are discussing.

- **Connecting People and Ideas:** I believe that things happen for a reason because we are all connected. I am able to see connection between seemingly disparate ideas. This supports my strategic thinking talent and assists me in identifying and developing relationships between others. Because I see connections that others often do not, others may see my ideas as being too "out there" and it often takes others time to process these connections before agreeing with my ideas. Sometimes, however, they just cannot see the connections and this can create frustration and tension.

Because of my unique themes of talent and abilities, my natural vocations are leadership, management, and consulting positions where my ability to see strategically, manage for maximum results, and drive action are valued and rewarded. In addition, my ability to find connections and continually learn allows me to add value in situations where growing networks and finding new information is needed and highly valued.

My Natural Way of Being Motivated

I am intrinsically motivated to action by…

- *Power:* I naturally enjoy being in a position where I can impact the lives of others in a positive way, and impact the value of organizations by directing and coaching the efforts of others. I also enjoy and excel at understanding and directing processes which lead to a maximization of positive results.

- *Affiliation:* I enjoy being appreciated for what I do and being part of something larger than myself.

Because of my natural way of being motivated, my natural vocations are leadership, management, consulting, and coaching positions where I can lead individuals and teams to success. In addition, I am naturally motivated to define, improve, and manage processes and the people who implement them. I also have a great desire to serve in leadership positions within non-profit organizations where my leadership skills will help grow these great organizations and in return, be highly valued by the organization. When taken to extreme, my need for power can be perceived as controlling or a "power trip." Therefore, I need to "soften" my direction and let others have control over "how" they get things done while I focus on the quality of the outcome.

My Unique Learning Style

My natural learning style is *auditory*, meaning that I learn best through active listening and my natural way of communicating is to "say it." I am also able to learn through "doing" (tactile) and visually, but I do not tend to communicate naturally or easily in these methods. This means that I am a natural speaker and a decent writer, but I must also be conscious and find ways to communicate my thoughts and ideas visually and provide instructions and practice for those who learn by doing. Understanding my learning style and natural way of communicating, I know I need to work with or employ others who have these natural strengths (tactile and visual) to help me communicate most effectively with people in my seminars and in my writings so I can best represent all learning styles.

If you have read this far, then you can quickly see that the process defined in this book, and thus my consulting practice in which it is based, is perfectly in alignment with my unique gifts. This alignment is not by accident. It is by design! The process defined in this book comes from using, with purpose and intent, my unique abilities to create something truly unique for myself and others, which I am now sharing with you in this book. It is important to note that this alignment did not happen overnight but came by honing my initial mission through purposeful and intentional action, review and revision. *So too can yours*!

Empowering or Limiting?

Before going to the next step, creating your Personal Mission Statement, it is important to stop here and consider what you think about the following question: "Is a Personal Profile a powerful tool or does it limit your power of choice?"

You have heard the conventional wisdom, "*You can be anything you want if you set your mind to it.*" In fact, during the visioning process we encouraged you to dream without bounds and quoted Napoleon Hill who said "*What the mind can conceive and believe, it can achieve.*" You may have heard that overcoming your weaknesses makes you stronger and more "well rounded." You may also be wondering if creating a Personal Profile will limit you to a few strengths and natural ways of being, and if this will limit your ultimate potential. These are all good questions and we believe we have a definitive answer!

We believe, without a doubt, that the Personal Profile is not only a powerful tool, but it is a true source of POWER. It is the center of your capabilities, but in no way does it limit your growth. It does, however, begin to paint your vision with that "brush of reality" we discussed earlier, and helps you understand that your vision and life's purpose are likely in alignment with your unique gifts.

The Personal Profile is much like an acorn. It is the seed upon which growth depends, but it does not limit you growing into a mighty oak. Taking this analogy one step further, if you are an acorn, it's not likely you will grow into a grape vine. Sure, you may work very hard and produce a few grape-looking-things along the way, but your true value and reward will be found when aligning yourself to your strengths so you can grow into that mighty, mighty oak and live to your full potential!

Creating a Personal Profile is empowering. It clearly defines and outlines who you are so you (and others) can understand what you have to work with so you can effectively make the decisions needed that will empower you to take the actions necessary so you can live the life of opportunity and personal fulfillment that you have dreamed of and defined.

A Personal Profile also gives you the foundation to create an effective "work-life integration," where all aspects of your life are effectively integrated, meshed, and aligned for optimum performance and personal fulfillment. We have all heard about "work-life balance," however, this term connotes a struggle between two separate worlds, *work* and *life*, where if one "wins," the other loses. With a Personal Profile outlining the unique gifts we bring to the table in all aspects of life, we have the tools to create a life where work not only supports and integrates with our family, our avocations, and our passions, but where work includes, supports and contributes to our passion, our family and our avocations. Without the clear understanding of who we are and our unique gifts provided by this Personal Profile, we are left to continually attempt to "balance" the ever moving teeter-totter between work and home life. Why not choose the more positive, empowering path?

When our clients embrace their unique gifts for the first time, and begin to act on the possibilities that come from a focus on those gifts, a light switch flips! A light of hope illuminates limitless potential! They experience real "ah-ha" moments, some very spiritual in nature and sincerely emotional. Often times, the dark curtains begin to part and our clients are introduced to a whole new world of opportunity. One they knew, intuitively, existed but had long given up. Now, however, they can act with confidence, using their known strengths and embrace the power and success that is theirs for the taking!

Now that you have completed your Personal Profile, it's time to create your Personal Mission Statement, your unique purpose.

Creating Your Personal Mission Statement

"Every man is said to have his peculiar ambition."
Abraham Lincoln

You now have in your possession a deeper and more complete understanding of the three important aspects of what makes you, YOU:

- Your unique themes of strengths, talents and abilities;

- Your natural learning style; and

- How you are uniquely intrinsically motivated.

As we have discussed previously, the more you are in alignment with these three aspects of what makes you – *you*, the more likely you will find happiness, personal fulfillment and success. As an example, think of a three-legged stool. What would happen if one leg were shorter than the other two, or if one leg was completely missing? You would have an unstable stool and it would be much safer to simply sit on the floor. Balance is necessary and

WHY it is important to know and understand your strengths as well as your learning and motivation styles.

Your Personal Passion

Take a look back at your vision statements. When you wrote about your career, did you note a pursuit of passion? Perhaps there is one hidden there. Perhaps you did not dare to state your passion because you thought it was impractical or because others have told you that it was crazy or unrealistic. Is there a burning desire stated there, or perhaps unstated?

If you know your passion, and you stated it in your vision, then you are deserving of significant congratulations! You are in rare territory, indeed. Usually, the first time out, very few people dare to state their true passion. So, if you already know your passion, you may find the Personal Mission Statement exercise fairly easy.

For the rest of us, however, finding our passion may require some additional self exploration. Everyone tells you to "*follow your dreams,*" or "*chase your passion,*" but you still need to know HOW to follow it, or even more fundamentally, HOW to discover it! We believe if you follow your passion, everything else will take care of itself. In other words, if you focus on finding and following your personal passion in your vocation, you will create or manifest the most likely situation for a happy and successful career, and coincidentally, the most likely conditions for a happy and fulfilling life.

How do you find your passion? Passion in life is found when you are inspired from within. You are more likely to be inspired from within when your vocation is in alignment with your strengths, learning style, and intrinsic motivation. You might not know today what your passion is, however, if you pursue work in alignment with your strengths, learning style, and intrinsic motivation, you will create a situation where you are most likely to find it. This is our belief and we've seen it proven time and time again.

Remember, Ben B., one of our clients first mentioned in the Introduction who discovered he was aligned to "coaching?" But coaching little league didn't pay the bills. He discovered, with further reflection on his strengths, that the art of coaching can be found in many professions, including financial planning, where he eventually excelled. Another client example is a young man, Greg L., whose strengths, natural inquisitiveness, made almost any profession seem interesting, causing him to bounce from job to job. After about a year of using these tools he discovered that, although anything might catch his attention for a brief period of time, only those jobs and activities where real inspiration and creativity were needed would create lasting and sustaining fulfillment for him. He is now well on his way to finding a true passion in his vocation in an inspiring and creative working environment.

So, even if you do not know – YET – what you are truly passionate about doing and do not believe – YET – that you have found your "true calling" in life, you will most likely find it by aligning yourself with these true aspects of who you are. This alignment is found through the development of a Personal Mission Statement.

As we have discussed, your Personal Mission Statement tells everyone what you do, who you serve, and how you provide value in the world. It is intended to be a clear and compelling statement of your life's passion and true calling. It is also a living statement, ever changing as you learn and grow, and something you will refer back to often. It is an extension of who you are, in the written word.

Where Are You Now?

After completing the exercises and your Personal Profile in the previous chapters, you are likely to find yourself in one of three places...

- The exercises confirmed what you already knew about yourself and clarified what you are interested in pursuing, or have always had a sense for pursuing. That is, you are now fairly certain where your strengths, learning style, and motivation align and you can't wait to get started; or

- The exercises have helped you narrow your choices, but you are still not 100% certain yet. You have developed some very good ideas and options that feel good and sound right to you, but you are not ready to commit to only one. Further testing and exploration is needed, and you are eager to begin; or

- You are still fairly uncertain. You see a number of ideas and many possibilities but just don't have that level of confidence to boldly step out and choose one path or to even explore a few options.

Regardless of where you are, it is OK if you are not yet 100% clear. If you are, great! But if not, then the most important thing you can take from all you have learned about yourself in the last few chapters of this book is this... There are hundreds, perhaps thousands of careers, pursuits, and jobs you can now be *certain* are NOT your life's passion and that your life's passion is almost certainly in alignment with those three aspects of who you are that you have now more clearly identified.

You have narrowed the search from the entire universe of everything imaginable to a manageable number of likely possibilities. Instead of having the daunting task of considering absolutely "everything," you now at least have a likely direction in which to start your search. If you have been paralyzed ("stuck") not knowing which way to go, you no longer need to be. You now have narrowed the playing field.

Keep in mind you may not know your true calling until you have actually experienced it for a while – by living it. You may have a pretty good idea of what you want to do, but until you actually do it, you may not be absolutely certain. And that is OK too! At least now you don't have to try hundreds of careers, just a few you know are more in alignment with your true self. And the likelihood that you will enjoy the work as you test and explore, even though you may discover it's not your true calling, is also fairly high.

If you still don't have a clear feel for that one true calling, take heart. It is extremely rare to know this for an absolute certainty, right out of the chute. But knowing what you know now after completing these exercises and having some likely possibilities in your court, puts you in the top 10-15% of the people in this world who have *direction*, and that is a heck of an advantage! Moving in that direction will continue to open up possibilities and opportunities you may not have even considered which will lead you toward identifying and living your passion.

If you know, or have a pretty good idea of your desired career choice or your true calling, then skip to the exercise: Drafting Your Personal Mission Statement, beginning on page 194, however, if you want to try to narrow it down a little further, then the following exercise will help you.

Narrowing Your Vocational Choices

If you feel the need to narrow your vocational options, answer the following questions and write them down as you go through each one:

- When you review your strengths, what careers (such as becoming a pharmaceutical rep) or lifestyle choices (such as a stay at home parent to home school your children) do they suggest to you?

- When you review your learning styles, what careers more naturally align to this way of processing information?

- What types of work does your natural way of being motivated suggest to you?

- What type of work environment would be needed to naturally motivate you? Would you work alone? Work with others? Manage a team?

- Do you see any overlaps or common themes? What are they?

- Are these common themes in alignment with your experience and the work you do or have enjoyed in the past?

- Are these common themes in alignment with your initial vision statement? In what way are they aligned? In what way are they not?

If there is alignment with your initial vision statements, then the vocational choice is likely the best path for you! Your instincts or basic desires were used to develop your vision statement while logic and assessment are the basis of the strengths, learning style, and motivation exercises. Bottom line, go with your gut, listen to that inner voice, and move toward your dreams!

Drafting Your Personal Mission Statement

To review, a Personal Mission Statement tells the world three things... What you do, who you serve, and what value you provide. Begin by answering the following three questions and list your answers on a separate piece of paper or on a white board:

- **What do you do?** Do you write, act, paint, calculate, consult, help, build, think, create, or communicate? What is the product or service associated with your unique gifts? Do you produce books, create paintings, develop reports, construct buildings, or bring people together? Do you provide guidance or assistance? Write down all the ideas that fit with your strengths, learning style, motivation, values and vision. Prioritize them by asking this question: If I live my entire life and never achieve _____, my life will not have been satisfying? You can review your strengths themes and the learning style and motivation exercises to find words that have meaning to you to assist you in answering these questions.

- **Who do you serve?** Think about who wants, uses, or buys your unique gifts, your product or service. Is it an individual? Women? Men? Your children? What age group? Or is it a corporation who would buy your services or products? What type of business? Large? Small? What industry? Who would value your product or service? Who would buy it? Keep in mind, "serving" doesn't necessarily have a monetary value. This section for you could mean identifying *who* would appreciate your volunteer contributions (such as a church or food bank), or *who* would benefit from your attention and teachings (such as your co-workers or your children).

- **What value do you provide?** Do you help people in their daily lives? Do you help them eat more healthfully, live more effectively, have better relationships? Do you help companies prosper and grow, find clarity, or develop talent? Do you help them account for their money, or find new markets?

  TIP: For Visual learners, look through magazines to find words or pictures of things that represent what you do, who you serve, and the value you provide, and cut them out so you can put them in a notebook or post them on a vision board.

TIP: For Kinesthetic learners, write these things on small pieces of paper so you can manipulate them... Or, as above, find pictures that you can manipulate.

TIP: For Auditory learners, you likely have little trouble brainstorming words; but if you do, try reading your Personal Profile out loud so you can "hear" the hidden gems.

Now that you have the three components of your mission statement (what you do, who you serve, and what value you provide), let's work to put it all together in a cohesive sentence or paragraph. It really does not matter which one you note first in the sentence. That is your preference. What is important is *clarity*. Your Personal Mission Statement needs to be clear - to you - and it needs to be clear to anyone who reads it.

Here are two examples, including my own Personal Mission Statement *(in italics, below):*

Example One: My Personal Mission Statement: I was able to clarify my personal mission statement after developing my Personal Profile (see page 180), and after discovering that my natural themes of talents and abilities were perfectly in line with the desire to enhance my coaching practice. In addition, my learning style is Auditory, so I enjoy talking, speaking and communicating with my clients. My natural motivation is Power (institutional) so I am naturally motivated to help others achieve. Defining this mission statement launched my business, Ottum Enterprises, the *Personal Growth Challenge*™, and this book.

"My unique purpose is to use my natural ability to sort through chaos to challenge adults to create a simple, clear, and compelling strategy and plan of action that allows them to act with confidence to maximize their growth and potential, to reach their personal and business objectives, to improve their relationships, and intentionally create the life they desire so they can achieve their dreams."

Although a relatively long run-on sentence, this statement clearly identifies my passion for helping others live their dreams.

Example Two: The following mission statement is from a woman, Debra B., introduced earlier in the book. Debra was in her 50's, a telecommunications consultant, and had always known there was something else she really wanted to do. She struggled to find her passion all her life. She thought she knew it, but her strengths actually caused her to be too conservative to risk it (her strengths taken to extreme became her weakness). Debra re-discovered that she had always wanted to own a dress shop, but not just any dress shop, one with real purpose that provided value beyond clothes. After going through *The Personal Growth Challenge*™ process, she was able to confidently move toward her dream – and so she did! Here is her finalized Personal Mission Statement:

"I provide a place for women to feel good about themselves. This includes a clothing store where women of all ages can find a good fit and a good value. And it includes a coffee shop and book store adjacent to the clothing store where women can gather, share information, and find the resources they need to better themselves."

Remember, as you draft your Personal Mission Statement keep your strengths in mind. They can actually be part of the statement, as these examples show.

Implementing Your Personal Mission Statement

A few tips to help you as you finalize or begin to implement your Personal Mission Statement:

- Keep in mind that one of the great things about the world we live in is that you can make a living at just about anything you set your mind to and potentially become wealthy while exercising your passion. As long as it is legal, in alignment with your values, and does not hurt others, you can express your passion within a chosen career any way you like.

- On the other hand, if you are struggling to apply your true passions to your vocation, you may want to consider creating two personal mission statements. One focused solely on your career, and the other focused on your outside interests. Your *vocation* is your job, career or business. It is how you make a living. Your *avocations* are your hobbies and interests.

They are how you have fun and recreate. The ideal, but not the requirement, is to have your work and career in alignment with your true passions. But that may not be possible or practical for you, and that is just fine!

- What is vital to remember is there are no generic right answers that work for everyone, only the answers that are right for you - right now. Let's say that again and give you time to think about this. The ONLY answers that matter are those answers that are right for you – right now.

- Living to your own Personal Mission Statement is not about conforming to someone else's notion of success. It is about defining your own success, in your own terms, and focusing on what you desire so you can create your life with intent, every day! So relax, if the process you have gone through to this point has not created absolute clarity today, it will come. It simply means you are not ready yet, but you will be. You likely have, however, a clearer direction and one that is more likely to lead you to the answers you seek.

- You will have plenty of time, the entire rest of your life in fact, to find that one true purpose. But even if you don't find it now, or even five years from now, you will likely have more fun, more fulfillment, and more success while working to find it after clearly defining and aligning your life to your unique gifts.

The Personal Mission Statement helps you find and pursue your purpose. Again, if your purpose is still not absolutely clear to you, that's OK! That is simply a continued challenge on your personal journey toward discovery. You will get there by consistently working the *Personal Growth Challenge*™ process. If you desire further assistance, you can find additional tools and suggestions for *living* your Personal Mission Statement on our website, *www.LivefromStrength.com*.

Summing Up Your Personal Strategic Foundation

Through the series of exercises, self reflection, and review, you now have three powerful tools:

- A clear and compelling **Personal Vision** of the life of your dreams that provides a clear direction for your life.

- A defined and written set of **Personal Values** that will guide your decisions.

- A **Personal Mission Statement** that will give your life purpose, meaning and defines what you do, for whom you do it, and the unique value you provide the world.

Together, these tools create a solid foundation on which you can build and live your dreams, each and every day. Through your Personal Strategic Foundation you have a unique purpose and now know the value you bring to the world, you have the tools to decide where you are going in life and the moral compass to guide your way. In Section III we will show you how to review and revise your vision, mission, and values to keep them fresh and make changes as you experience more and learn more about yourself.

You now know where you are going in your life, but now it is time to assess where you are today. Every life journey must start at exactly the same place; *where you are right now.* In order to chart the right course you must first define your starting point and honestly assess where you are now against your Personal Strategic Foundation (where you want to go). Doing so will allow you to more easily assess how far you have grown when you consider the progress you have made along the way, which we begin to discuss on page 285.

Section II:
Assessing Where You Are Today

"Rather than love, than money, than fame, give me truth."
Henry David Thoreau

"I made my own assessment of my life, and I began to live it.
That was freedom."
Fernando Flores

Knowing Where You Are Today

"Self assessment is universal truth."
Unknown

When you look at making changes in your life, or moving in a new direction toward your vision, before you can build your Personal Annual Action Plan you must first understand where you are today, right now, in this moment. When traveling, there is always a destination and a place of departure - a starting point. Knowing your starting point allows you to determine how far you must travel and in what direction you must go to get to your intended destination. And then, of course, you must consider the "mode" of transportation. If you can't take a train or an airplane from where you live, you might have to drive to your first destination in order to catch a train to jump on a plane to get to your ultimate destination. Right? So it is with your own life's journey toward your vision.

An assessment of your starting point, therefore, must consider two things to put the proper context into building a plan of action:

- **Assess Your "Current State" to determine where you are today**, right now, in relation to your Personal Strategic Foundation (vision, mission and values). Without knowing your starting point and just how far you are from your destination, how can you define your course of action or the best path to get there?

- **Determine what you must "do" or "change" to get there** in order to achieve your vision, activate on your mission, and live your values. In other words, you must determine whether you take a train, a plane, or an automobile, and in what order, to get where you want to go. The similar concept for your life's journey is to know what you must do to reach your goals and what obstacles (real or imagined) stand between you and where you want to go.

So, how do you assess where you are today, and WHAT do you assess? Those are the questions that tend to stump most people and keep them stuck in the same rut day after day, year after year. Fortunately, your answers to these questions will come to you easier because of the work you have already accomplished while developing your Personal Strategic Foundation. You simply evaluate yourself today in relation to how you have defined each of the components of your foundation! The important point here is that your Personal Strategic Foundation defines the life you want to live and you explore these areas to assess your current state, as follows:

- **Assessing Your Vision:** Since your vision defines your direction and future destination, it makes it easier to assess how far you are from it, and which direction you must go to achieve it. For now, ask yourself this question, *"Where am I today in relation to the life I want to live?"* Are you close and it's just around the corner? Are you so far away you can barely see the light in the distance? Either or any answer is OK. The important thing is that you develop an honest and realistic understanding of where you are today and how far you need to go.

- **Assessing Your Values:** A little less obvious is assessing where you are toward your personal values. We all would like to believe we live our values daily, right now! But for most of us, we have never really defined them in detail as you did in the values exercises while developing your Personal Strategic Foundation. It's important to understand what changes we need to make to be able to live our values each and every day. The question to ask yourself is, *"How well do I live these values now, today, each and every day?"* Do you never waiver? Do you struggle? If so, why? It could be that the value you're struggling with isn't a good fit for you, or it needs to be more clearly defined.

- **Assessing Your Mission:** The Personal Strategic Foundation you created also defines your life's purpose through your Personal Mission Statement.

This defines how you will provide value to the world so the universe, in turn, can provide for you and your family in abundance. Some of us may be fully activating on the Personal Mission Statement we defined right now, but most of us have a little, perhaps even a lot of work to do to get there. So the questions are, *"Am I living my life's purpose today? If not, what needs to be done in order to start living my desired life of purpose?"*

In short, the only important things to consider about your life today are those things related to your Personal Strategic Foundation. There is no need to assess your past, or obsess about the future. You only need to be concerned with where you are today, in this moment, in relation to the life you have now defined for yourself. There is no need to understand and assess any rules or ways of life that others may impose on you. You need only evaluate those you have defined for yourself. In that vein, there is no need to consider your skills and capabilities for your current job or profession, unless it is already in alignment with your unique purpose. You do, however, need to assess where you are toward truly using your strengths and natural learning and motivation styles to determine how to most effectively activate on your Personal Mission Statement.

The Personal Strategic Foundation is the definition of you - the real you - and the life of purpose, direction and integrity you have always dreamed of. *There is nothing else to consider.* Your Personal Strategic Foundation is of utmost importance to you as it encompasses *everything of value* to you in your life! So the only thing worth assessing, now or at any time in the future, is your current state with regard to your current vision, your Personal Mission Statement, and your values.

How do you go about it? In the next few sections we will show you a simple and effective way to assess where you are today - or at any time in the future. In fact, this is a terrific tool to use to assess why you might be feeling a little "off" or "not right" about yourself at any time. We have found that by using this tool you can quickly determine the problem, develop an action plan to re-align yourself, and begin to feel "right" again in as little as 15 minutes! This ability is another reason why there is so much POWER when you *Live from Strength!*

Assessing Your Current State

The first part of the assessment is to determine how close or how far you are from having or living your vision, mission, and values. To determine this you literally, and quite simply, rate each line of the Personal Strategic Foundation, one by one, on a scale of 1 to 10 where...

- **1 means:** *"I have not begun to achieve this desire,"* or *"I do not live this day-to-day."* That is, you have always wanted this aspect of your vision, but have not done anything about it. Or you have always meant to live a certain way, such as healthfully, but do not. Finally, it may mean you have always wanted to live your passion, as stated in your Personal Mission Statement, but have not taken the necessary steps to move toward it (i.e., you haven't taken classes or worked in the field, etc.).

- **10 means:** *"I have this now,"* or *"I live this every day."* A rating of 10 means you already achieved that aspect of your vision or you consistently, and without fail, live that aspect of your values. Or it may mean you are currently at the full potential of your Personal Mission Statement and are receiving abundance from the universe in return for the value you are providing.

As an example, let's take a look at your vision. You have a number of statements, from financial to relationships, to community connections. Our example client, Mary, said something like the following in her personal vision about her health:

"I am at my ideal weight of 125 pounds. I am healthy and fit and I feel great about my appearance. I maintain my weight, fitness level, and appearance by exercising four to five times per week, including walking, dance, and yoga."

Mary can rate this vision statement in one of two ways. She can rate it as a whole, assessing the totality of the statement, rating herself using the above scale of 1 to 10. But this single vision statement is actually several distinct concepts, so she can choose to rate each one separately. If this is your vision statement, to analyze your statement more deeply, you would first assess the sentence regarding your weight. Where are you toward that vision or goal for yourself? Be completely honest with yourself. Next, you might independently assess your health and your fitness. Then you would rate how you feel about your appearance. Do you exercise to maintain a healthy weight? How often and how effectively or strenuously do you exercise? Finally, are you doing those activities you enjoy? Are you walking, dancing, and taking yoga classes?

We make this point to show that with each statement there are usually multiple concepts. For some of your stated concepts you may be doing very well, while others you may not have begun at all or you are doing them inconsistently. Assessing your foundation in this way helps you to truly understand each concept and validate it once again, helping to sharpen and hone your vision, values, and personal mission statement. This process also helps make it clear to yourself those things that need more attention in order to ultimately get where you want to go in your life so you can be who you want to be.

Whichever way you choose to assess your current state, the important point of the assessment is to be truly - and sometimes brutally - honest with yourself and let the chips fall where they may. It is truly OK if your assessment shows mostly numbers below 5. That simply means you're being honest with yourself and have a few things to work on. The ratings to question are the ones where you assess yourself with 9's and 10's. At that point you may be deluding yourself into thinking you are better off than you really are, or you may have simply set the bar way too low for yourself. Remember, this is an introspective process and may be a challenge to complete. This is why we call our consulting service the *Personal Growth Challenge*™. Further, once you achieve 10's across the board you will want to set new goals for yourself and expand your vision. Having ratings lower than 10 right now is a good thing. It gives you something to work toward. By setting your sights on *becoming* all 10's you will be naturally driven toward the life of your dreams!

Now it is time to actually do the assessment. Look at each line of your vision statement, your values, and your mission statement, and rate each one on a scale of 1 to 10. Your results will likely have a mixture of ratings below 5, between 5 and 8, and a few 9's or 10's. Again, the results are not important, however, an honest assessment is. Document your answers next to each statement, sentence, or concept.

Assessing Change

Now that you have assessed how close or how far you are from living the life you have envisioned for yourself, it's time to determine what you need to do, need to change, or need to do differently in order to rate yourself a

9 or 10 in those areas rated lower. That is, you want to assess what needs to be different in your life in order to have and live your vision, consistently live to your values, and to be fully executing on your Personal Mission Statement.

You will assess change for ONLY those items rated with an 8 or less. The reason you don't evaluate those given a 9 or a 10 is because 10 is perfection and many of us believe no one is perfect and tend not to give a rating of 10. And, 9 is pretty darn close! Celebrate those things you are doing well. Typically, we beat ourselves up enough for our non-perfections, so pat yourself on the back for those things rated a 9 and focus only on those things that truly need positive action.

To assess change, ask three simple questions of yourself for each item you rated 8 or less. The questions are:

- "If I were to rate _____ (fill in the blank) a 9 or 10, what would I have to start doing right now that I am not doing today?" In other words, what are the things you are not currently doing that would be required to live or have what you desire. Would you need to start studying a trade? Would you need to begin an exercise program or change your diet? Would you need to get more involved in your community or a social group?

- "If I were to rate _____ (fill in the blank) a 9 or 10, what would I have to continue doing that I am currently doing today?" It is likely you are already doing many things that are in alignment with your Personal Strategic Foundation. What are they? Are you exercising a few times a week? Are you eating healthfully? Are you in school already, or teaching yourself Spanish?

- "If I were to rate _____ (fill in the blank) a 9 or 10, what would I have to STOP doing that I am currently doing today?" This is perhaps the most important question of the three. We are usually taught to consider what we are doing or what we need to do that leads us to our objectives, but we rarely consider those things we are doing that are impeding our progress. Things that you need to consider here are: negative thoughts, bad habits, poor behaviors, or inappropriate actions you are currently doing that are not in alignment with your newly defined Personal Strategic Foundation. As an example, if one of your values is being "impeccable with my word," then participating in negative gossip about a co-worker, or swearing profusely at a sporting event while surrounded by people of all ages is not truly living to your stated value. So you would list "stop gossiping" and "stop swearing" as the things you need to stop doing. Later in the process (beginning on page 265), we will show you how to turn these negative statements into positive affirmations such as, "I find positive things to say about my co-workers and friends," or "I use positive, clean, and professional language."

The following three questions are the cornerstone for making positive change toward becoming the vision of yourself you have defined:

What do I need to **start** doing?

What do I need to **continue** doing?

What do I need to **stop** doing?

Your answers to these three questions tell you what you are doing well, what you need to begin doing, and as importantly, what you need to stop doing so you can become the person you want to be and live the life you truly desire.

An Example

Let's look at this a little more closely and take a peek at what our example client, Mary, rated for herself on the following:

- *I am at my ideal weight of 125 pounds.* With this statement, Mary rated herself a 6 because she is currently 134 pounds. Mary knows in order to be at - or near - her ideal weight she would need to...

- *Start* eating more fruits and vegetables, eating more fish and lean meats, and eating five small meals a day, or using the stairs instead of the elevator, or any number of healthier activities or ideas that work best for her.

- *Continue* to exercise and eat healthfully, taking her own lunch to work, or any healthy activities and habits she is currently doing.

- *Stop* eating junk food, eating lunch out, drinking sugary lattes every morning, putting butter on everything, drinking alcohol in excess, or any number of un-healthy activities she might be doing. The counter-positive to these negative statements could be, *"I eat healthfully, drink in moderation, and participate in activities I enjoy to keep me active, healthy, and fit."*

- *I am healthy and fit and I feel great about my appearance.* Mary rated herself a 5 here as she feels she has a few health issues and is not as fit as she would like to be. In addition, she doesn't feel as good about her appearance as she would like. So in addition to the things she must start, continue, and stop doing that she listed above, she might:

  - *Start* seeing and visualizing herself as healthy and fit and see a doctor for her health issues, or work with a counselor to help with self-esteem issues, or engage a life coach or stylist. She may also begin working on her closet, cleaning out those clothes that fit poorly so she has room for clothes that do bring out the best in her each day.

- *Continue* to buy and wear clothes that make her look and feel good or continue any number of activities or habits she is currently doing that help her to feel better about herself and her appearance.

- *Stop* thinking of herself as fat and out of shape and stop any and all negative thoughts about her health and appearance by turning these negative thoughts into the counter positives, such as *"I am fit, in shape and healthy, and I look and feel great!"*

• *I maintain my weight, fitness and appearance by exercising four to five times per week, including walking, dance and yoga.* Mary rated herself a 7 as she does exercise a few times a week, perhaps not as strenuously as she could, and she occasionally takes a yoga class and goes out dancing with friends on the weekends. Here, in addition to those things above, she might...

- *Start* taking a regular dance class, using a personal trainer, taking walks at lunch, or increasing the intensity of her workouts.

- *Continue* to take yoga classes and exercising regularly.

- *Stop* socializing during her workouts so she can focus and make them more effective. Can you formulate the counter-positive statement here? Give it a shot!

Does all this sound a bit simplistic? Good! The simpler the better! We love to use our KISS theory... *Keep It Simple Solutions!* As we have discussed, becoming the person you want to be, and living the life you truly want is not about making broad, sweeping changes that are hard to implement and even harder to sustain. It's about making a series of small, incremental changes that stick with you in the long run. Have you ever heard this expression before, *"How do you eat an elephant? – One bite at a time!"* Literally and figuratively, it's true!

Now, look at your list again in your Personal Strategic Foundation for ratings lower than 9 or 10 and ask yourself what you would need to *start, continue* and *stop* doing, right now in order to give yourself a rating of 9 or 10. Go ahead, we'll wait for you to finish. Just come back when you're done and we will move on to the next part of the assessment.

Below is one way to organize your assessment using a spreadsheet:

Statement	Rating (1-10)	Start	Continue	Stop
List vision, mission and value statements here.	Place 1-10 rating here.	List items to start here.	List items to continue here.	List items to stop here.

Prioritizing Your Assessment

Once you have rated your level of attainment in your Personal Strategic Foundation and then determined what you have to *start*, *continue*, and *stop* doing, right now, to achieve your desired ratings in those areas, it is time to prioritize.

"Prioritize," you ask? "Isn't every single line in my Personal Strategic Foundation as important as the other? Wasn't that the purpose of doing it in the first place - to get to the essence of what is absolutely important to the life I want to live?" Well, yes, with one caveat. You can have anything you defined in your Personal Strategic Foundation, but you cannot always have everything you want instantly or all at the same time. This is another opportunity to paint your vision with a brush of current reality so that you can focus on implementing a small, manageable and prioritized number of changes, rather than trying to change everything at once.

Also, prioritization does not absolutely mean that one thing is more important than another. Instead, it may imply that one thing must happen in order to achieve another. For example, you may need to activate on your personal mission to achieve your financial goals. Or the opposite may be true. You may need to achieve a certain financial position in order to launch a business before you can activate your personal mission.

Prioritization also helps you transition to *action* by helping you be very clear on what you need to do to achieve your goals and live the life you truly desire.

When you prioritize the items in your Personal Strategic Foundation, you look at three concepts: the *relative importance* of each item; the *relative urgency* of each item; and the *relative order of accomplishment* of each item. Let's look at these in more detail.

Importance

The *relative importance* of the items in your personal vision, values, and mission is, quite simply, a ranked order based on the importance they have to you. Again, there are no right answers - only the answers that are right for you. *Why* they are important is not the issue. What you *feel* is most important *is*. This is all about your *emotional* attachment to that aspect of the life you are building.

To rank importance, you can simply go through each item and rank the various statements in your Personal Strategic Foundation in order from one to whatever. Look through the list asking yourself which item is (or feels) most important to you. That item is number one. You repeat the process to rank the second most important, then the third, and so on. Using this method, you may find it difficult to differentiate those items at the top and bottom of the list. If that is the case, you might use a method similar to the one you used to rank order your values. That is, go through the list and ask yourself which are most important and critical to you and mark those with an A. Those that are important, but not critical give a B. And mark those that are somewhat important a C.

Another way to rank importance is to ask which of the items, if you never started or completed, would you feel most disappointed about if you never achieved them or experienced them in your life. Again, this is about emotion - not logic. Which of the items in your Personal Strategic Foundation touch you emotionally or create an emotional reaction or spark when you read them? These likely have the most *importance* to you. If you do not know why, spend a few moments trying to understand your emotional reaction. This includes clearly understanding what emotion is being elicited (fear vs. elation vs. hope vs. deep desire, etc.) and try to understand why you have an emotional reaction (you fear failing at this, you have always believed this to be your destiny, etc.).

So now, take a few minutes to review your Personal Strategic Foundation and rank order each item in importance in a way that makes the most sense to you.

Using the spreadsheet method we introduced earlier, you would add a column for importance, as follows:

Statement	Rating (1-10)	Start	Continue	Stop	Import
List vision, mission and value statements here.	Place 1-10 rating here.	List items to start here.	List items to continue here.	List items to stop here.	Place rating 1-X here.

Urgency

Similar to importance, urgency is an emotional, not a logical ranking. Urgency is about which items you feel you need to take action on – *right now*. Which items do you feel you need to take care of right when you wake up tomorrow morning? It is about which items make you feel most anxious to get started or get done!

Now, take your Personal Strategic Foundation, starting from the most to least important, and rate the urgency you have to getting started or achieving it. Also spend a few moments to attempt to understand why you feel this urgency. Is it because you have been itching to do this all your life? Is it because somebody has told you that you can't or won't be able to do it because you're not old enough, not young enough, or smart enough? Is it because this is truly what you want, or is it because of some other outside influence? The point here is to resist placing urgency on items when it does not come from within you, when it is truly not in alignment with who you are. Urgency comes from a burning desire within you, from a place of internal inspiration, not from anger, or resentment, or a place outside yourself, or from someone else's influence or desire for you.

Now rate the relative urgency of your vision, mission and value statements by adding a column for Urgency to your assessment spreadsheet.

Order

Now that we have looked at prioritization from an emotional standpoint, it is time to look at things from a *logical* perspective. Putting order to the achievement of the items in your personal vision, values, and mission statements means determining which items are fundamental to the achievement of other items in your list - and need to be fulfilled or acted on first in order to achieve the rest.

As we discussed, you may need to reach a particular financial position before activating on a business idea. Or you may need to put a certain aspect of your values in place to gain the respect and appreciation needed to advance your career. For many, getting training, education, or additional experience is required to activate on a personal mission.

The first thing to consider when reviewing order is to validate your emotional desire for urgency. Look at the items you ranked high in urgency. Ask yourself if any other required aspects of your foundation are needed to make these urgent items come about? If there are, make a note of those thoughts next to the item. For example, you may feel an urgency to make a certain income because of pressing financial issues. This may require, however, that you fully implement your personal mission through a different career.

Next, assess those items you ranked as most important. Are there other aspects of your foundation that need to be in place to achieve these more important items? Again, if so, make a note next to that item. For example, it may be important for you to have healthy and positive relationships with family or friends, as stated in your vision; however, to do this, you may need to first better live your value of "open and honest communication" as a necessary step toward making those relationships better.

Finally, let's look at another aspect that might impact order. For the most part, achievement of all aspects of your vision and the activation of your personal mission are dependent upon the development of your talents into strengths. Remember, a talent must be developed into a strength through the acquisition of knowledge and the development of skill. Thus, if you are to attain all that you want and fully activate on your Personal Mission Statement, the acquisition of knowledge and the focused practice and exercise to develop those skill(s) - are priorities.

Now, review your Personal Strategic Foundation one last time and look for items that are dependent on the development of your strengths. Naturally, your Personal Mission Statement is one, so list out the knowledge and skills needed to achieve it. Do you need to obtain a college degree, which might be part of another aspect of your foundation, such as your vision? Do you need specific work experience or a career change? Which items are dependent on another and thus require a certain order? Now, review the other aspects of your foundation (vision and values). Are there others that are dependent on the development of your strengths? What knowledge and skills are required? For example, to become a more effective manager, you may need to develop your strengths of Command, Strategy or Empathy. Alternatively, you may desire to be a better parent, however, you realize that to be the parent you desire to be you must first manage your strengths of Command and need for Achievement to mitigate taking those strengths to extreme and being perceived by your children as overly bossy, manipulative and focused too much on getting things done.

Now rate the relative order of your vision, mission and value statements. If you are using the spreadsheet method, add another column to the spreadsheet and place your rating in the column.

Creating Your Prioritized List

Once you have completed the assessment, take all the items you listed and put them into a master prioritized list, from highest to lowest. If you used the spreadsheet method, one way to create the prioritized list is to create one last column where you score each item from 1-10 based on the relative importance, urgency and order. This "master score" will naturally rank the items from highest to lowest priority when you sort the data based on the numbers in this column. If at any point you don't know which one is the higher prioritized item, go with your gut. Go with what *feels* right to you.

Often times we find that clients can effectively see (or feel) the relative prioritized order of their top five to 10 items. After that, however, most of the items on their list all seem to feel about the same and they find it difficult to discern measureable differences between items 12 and 19, for example. If this happens to you, it is both normal and good for one very important reason! That is, it validates that those items on the top are truly THE most important items in your life right now and the rest, well, they aren't and so you can stop stressing about them! Whew!

Once complete, you will use this list to take action on your top priority items, the items that DO matter to you. For examples of completed prioritized lists, visit our website at *www.LivefromStrength.com.*

What Does This Assessment Mean?

Let's take a look at what this assessment information means and figure out how we can use it to take action.

First, you assessed how close or how far you are from living your Personal Strategic Foundation by assigning a number from 1 to 10, where 10 is, "I live it now," or "I have it now," and 1 is, "I have not even started." For those items you rated a 9 or 10, congratulations! You are already living the life of your dreams in those areas! This should definitely be celebrated! For the others, those are the items for which you need to build an action plan to achieve.

In order to build that action plan, you already answered some basic questions. That was, "*In order to be living, or to have these items right now, what would I have to start, continue, and stop doing?*" Your answers to these questions gave you a basic list of things you are currently doing well, some things you need to start doing, and as importantly, a list of things you need to stop doing, right now!

But not all of these things can be had "right now." Most need to be worked on over time. So which do you work on first? In this regard, you prioritized those items and you created a list from highest to lowest priority. You first prioritized by how important they are to you. You then prioritized them by timing, both in terms of emotional urgency, and in terms of logical order. For the latter, you considered the need to develop your strengths as a priority, as achievement of much of your Personal Strategic Foundation will be dependent on the full expression of these strengths.

As a result of this process, you now have a number of ways to help you answer the question, *"What do I do NOW to begin to achieve my dreams?"*

What you do now is *take action!* Targeted, focused, and directed action! But as humans, though remarkable as we are, we have a difficult time doing lots of things at once.

We need *focus*. Think of it this way. Most highly trained professional jugglers can only keep three to five balls in the air at a time consistently. Trying to juggle many things at once is naturally difficult. We need to focus on a relatively short list of *THE* most important priorities. Given that, your assessment has helped you begin to see where you are in your journey, what actions you need to take, and which actions you need to do *first* in order to get where you want to go.

Now, your next step is to take your Personal Strategic Foundation and your list of priorities and build your Personal Annual Action Plan. But first, since much of your action may cause or require "changes" in your life to enable you to live in alignment with your Personal Strategic Foundation, let's take a few moments to talk about *change*.

About Change

In the book, *The Hundred Year Lifestyle*, author Dr. Eric Plasker discusses a great theory that got us thinking... *"Change is easy... **thinking** about change is hard."*

At first we thought this a rather trite expression but as we continued to analyze it, we found it to be an extremely powerful and important message as to why so many of us struggle to take action for positive change in our life, or we simply give up shortly after we start and, consequently, fall short in our attempts to change. After completing your Current State Assessment, you may be wondering just how you are going to make all of these positive changes. It is a common concern many of our clients have, for a number of good reasons.

NOTE: The following paragraphs may feel negative to you, and they are! We believe it is important to show you the limiting and negative way many people typically think about and deal with change. We will also show you a simple and powerful way to embrace change so you can

"Learn to embrace change, and you'll begin to recognize that life is in constant motion, and every change happens for a reason. When you see boundaries as opportunities, the world becomes a limitless place, and your life becomes a journey of change that always finds its way." Unknown

confidently take positive action to create the life of your dreams.

Typically when faced with change, especially significant change, we begin to create mental movies in our head with Oscar-winning performances depicting everything that can go wrong while worrying about all that we must do, all that we don't have, and all that is unknown, looped on a continuous reel that never ends.

That is, we "think" about change in the context of all that can go wrong, rather than making a conscious choice to focus on everything that can go right! It is no wonder so many people stay trapped in lives, jobs, and relationships that are actually destructive for them rather than choosing *change*. Sadly it seems more people are willing to "die" (so to speak) in their complacent, comfortable (known) existence rather than choosing the unknown path (change) to reach for what they really want in their life! Have you heard the expression, *"Better the devil you know than the devil you don't?"* It's that "devil" that keeps you stuck where you are, and we're here to tell you - *it's all in your head!*

In addition, we are often haunted by the past, even though we cannot change it. Often times, we believe our past is destined to rule our present reality and our future. We are what we are and we are the sum total of our past thoughts and actions, or so we are told. Though it is true we cannot change the past and we are, up to this point, the sum total of our past thoughts and actions, the question to ask yourself is; *what does this have to do with my ability to change and create a different future for myself now?*

When you woke up this morning, what power did the past have on what thoughts and actions you choose today? Really, in a word, NONE! Yes, you may not have completed your education, or have limited financial resources, or have made a few bad choices in your lifetime thus far, but they only limit you today because you allow them to. Eckart Tolle in his breakthrough work, *The Power of Now*, puts it this way, *"The only place where change can occur and the past can be dissolved is in the Now."* Your power for change is *now*, in this moment! Choices are ONLY made in the *now*, and thus *change* only happens in the now.

"Don't cry over spilled milk," we are told. *"Don't try to do tomorrow's work today."* All true, but these admonishments fail to emphasize the power and importance of what that leaves us! TODAY... this very moment! What is left is the decision right in front of us! What an extraordinarily powerful and wonderful gift when you think about change in that way, because that is all you have to think about... *this very moment*. Thus, to make change, any change, whether trivial or profound, you need only think about right now! Nothing more! What choice do you need to make, right now? What action do you need to take, right now?

Change happens only one way. One day, one action, one decision, one choice, and one step at a time, moment by moment. That's it! And, remember, doing nothing *IS* a choice. So, if you want to make changes in your life, you need only think about the one decision in front of you right now, in this moment and act. Simple and powerful!

Once you come to this realization, many of us experience fear that tries to keep us imprisoned and frozen in our own mind - before we even get started. That fear usually stems from not knowing *HOW?* with a big question mark! How do you make the right decisions? Do you continue using your old mental tapes (your practiced, but not necessarily healthy thought patterns), played in your head over and over, or consider what others think you should do, or what Mom or Dad always told you to do? Or will you use a set of tools that clearly and accurately defines who you are and who you really want to become? Do you toe the line and continue in your old (known) ways, or do you do what is in alignment with your true self that calls for you to step outside your somewhat comfortable (but non-aligned) box? Do you follow the masses, or do you follow your heart? Do you do what is right for others, or what is right for you? Take a few moments to let these questions sink in. Give yourself time to answer them honestly.

By developing your Personal Strategic Foundation, you now have a clearly defined purpose in life, a clear vision of where you want to go, and you know the values by which you want to live. So now, change really IS easy for you. It simply becomes a matter of asking if this one choice in front of you right now IS in alignment with who you are or wish to become, and then taking that one step now to act on it. That's it! If the choice in front of you is not in alignment with your authentic self, you simply discard it and move on to something that is. Change *can be* that easy.

Your Personal Strategic Foundation defines your alignment with your true self and provides you with the necessary tools to make the decision in front of you - right now! These tools will empower you to make that decision, and the next, and the next, without question or self-doubt. You will have the confidence to act, knowing that the decisions you make are in alignment with who you are. This powerful knowledge will keep you on your chosen path, day after day, year after year!

Change as a Process

Even armed with this power, it is still important to think about change as a gradual process, not something to be done overnight in leaps and bounds, and all right now. As an example, many of us may commit to an exercise program but give up soon after we start because our muscles get sore or the weight does not come off fast enough. We might try to quit smoking or drinking but then give up when we "fall off the wagon."

There are two important things to remember here:

- Case studies show people need anywhere from 22 to 30 days to form a new habit or break an old one. Keeping this in mind, true change will occur when you have successfully repeated the right decisions over a longer period of time.

- Nobody is perfect! You may make the wrong decisions on occasion, even armed with all the right tools. So give yourself a break! Forgive yourself if you fall, be kind to yourself, and consciously move on to the next decision and aim to do better! Get over it, get up, move on, and resolve to do better next time. There really is no need to wallow in bad feelings. Tomorrow brings a new day of opportunities. The important thing here is - now you have defined exactly what you can fall back on! You have your outlined "road map" if (on occasion) you stray from your chosen path.

Bottom line, you can relax about change. Change is easy when it is done one decision at a time! And truly, that's the only way it happens. Simply focus and ask yourself three questions:

- What can I do today to move me closer to my goals and vision?

- Is this choice in front of me right now, in alignment with my authentic self and the life I truly desire?

- How can I effectively use my strengths to accomplish this choice?

By keeping these three questions in mind as you go through each day, you will master change while you *Live from Strength.*

Section III:
Building a Personal
Annual Action Plan

"A clear vision, backed by definite plans, gives you a tremendous feeling of confidence and personal power."
Brian Tracy

"Whatever failures I have known, whatever errors I have committed, whatever follies I have witnessed in private and public life have been the consequence of action without thought."
Bernard Baruch, stock broker, advisor to Presidents Woodrow Wilson, and Harry S. Truman, (1870-1965)

Your Personal Annual Action Plan

"Planning is bringing the future into the present so that you can do something about it now."
Alan Lakein

To quickly summarize where you are in *The Personal Growth Challenge*™ process and in aligning your life to your strengths, let's do a quick review of what you have learned so far:

- You discovered in the introduction that a life well lived is defined by disciplined thought (a well defined strategy), an honest and comprehensive assessment of where you are now (a Current State Assessment), and disciplined action (as outlined in a plan, like a business plan).

- You have exercised disciplined thought and developed your strategy through the Personal Strategic Foundation. This includes a clear vision of the life you desire that will compel and propel you in a given direction. You have also defined your life's purpose, creating meaning and focus in your life. And you have created a set of values (your personal compass) that will guide your decision making along the way to your life's dreams.

- You have also assessed where you are today against that foundation and prioritized the results of that assessment to focus on those things that are most important and urgent to you - right now - and in what order they need to be done.

Now it is time for *ACTION!* Disciplined, purposeful, intentional, and glorious action! It is time to develop your Personal Annual Action Plan so you can *Live from Strength!*

Giving Up on Outcome

It is imperative to give up on *outcome* and focus on *ACTIVITY* in our action planning.

For most of us, what we desire, as defined in our vision and our goals, will take time to achieve. In some cases, it may take years with many expected and unexpected twists and turns along the way. We must take small steps toward our goals every day in manageable chunks of time in order to move closer to our dreams and truly experience the journey along the way.

It is necessary to focus today on the small steps that lead to our goals by giving up on outcomes and *believing* if we continue to do the right things we will live the life of our dreams with every step we take! The outcomes will come, one by one, over time as we focus on doing the day-to-day activities that are most likely going to get us where we want to go.

Action planning, therefore, is a dedicated focus of managing the activities that lead to success. Said another way, long-term success is achieved through a series of small, day-to-day successes strung together. Great success will come if you focus on the small, "bite-sized" successes each and every day.

As one of the deans of personal success, Earl Nightingale, once said, "Don't let the fear of the time it will take to accomplish something stand in the way of your doing it. The time will pass anyway; we might just as well put that passing time to the best possible use." Well said, indeed!

The steps of developing your Personal Annual Action Plan will guide you to take purposeful, focused action each day, but many of those daily actions will only be small, nearly invisible steps toward the ultimate objective, your Personal Vision. Therefore, it is necessary to let go of, or "give up" on outcome and trust that by focusing on those daily tasks you are one action, one day, and one step at a time, creating your life *on purpose*, with intent, and navigating your ship toward a life well lived.

Personal Annual Action Plan Components

A comprehensive and effective personal annual action plan to *Live from Strength,* which continually moves you toward the life you desire, has the following components:

- **A theme for the year.** This is a positive and fun statement of intent for the year. It is your major focus for *this* year. The one major concept, idea, or aspect of your life you choose to work on during this planning cycle (this year). It might be financial in nature, focus on building relationships, or just aligning yourself so you can consistently live your values. (Examples: *"This is my year to rejuvenate my mind and soul."* Or, *"This is my year to organize my life."*)

- **Goals and Objectives:** These are the defined milestones for the year that are focused on your top priorities. You will develop detailed action plans for each goal with clear measurements and timelines so you can keep yourself on track and re-tool or re-group if necessary when you feel off track. Also, we will give you some information to help you demystify and take the fear out of setting goals. We will help you look at goals and objectives differently so you can utilize them more effectively in your life in a way that works best for you.

- **Weekly Accomplishment Lists:** We recommend developing a weekly "to do" plan that lists the things you want to accomplish during the week. One week provides a far enough look into the future to purposefully schedule your time and accomplish significant chunks of activity, but short enough to effectively control the time without fear of significant changes to the plan or feeling overwhelmed. A monthly accomplishment plan is an alternative, and if that works better for you, that's OK as well. Or even a combination of the two. What is important is the act of translating the annual action plan into manageable and achievable activities that need to be done – in a way that works best for you.

- **Daily Action Plan:** It all comes down to today. It is really all we have to work with. You may have heard the quote, *"Yesterday is history. Tomorrow is a mystery. And today? Today is a gift. That's why we call it the present!"* Babatunde Olatunji, noted educator, social activist and recording artist, gave us this golden nugget. A similar version is also attributed to Alice Morse Earle, American historian and author. In other words, we only have power over our choices for this day, in this moment. So, what are you going to choose to do today, right now? We recommend creating a list of the top six things you need to do today (based on your Weekly Accomplishments List) that will not only move you toward the life you desire, but allow you to LIVE the life you desire today.

- **Positive Affirmations to Support Your Plan:** We recommend creating specific daily affirmations that support the theme and goals for your annual plan as well as other positive changes in thoughts, attitudes and behaviors which may be needed to manifest your Personal Strategic Foundation.

- **Periodic Status Reviews:** We recommend you review your progress toward your annual plan at least quarterly. You may feel the need to review more frequently if you have many short-term goals and objectives to ensure you are staying on track and meeting your stated goals. You may also need to review your plan when things change in your life. This could be something major - such as meeting that special someone, losing or starting a job, or suffering a loss of a pet or loved one. But also, you may need to review your status whenever you feel a "little off." Later in this section (see page 287) we will show you a powerful tool to use to check in with yourself and pinpoint where you might have gone astray so you can quickly get yourself back on track to feeling right aligned again!

Now it is time to break down each component into bite-sized pieces so we can guide you through developing your first action plan so you can *Live from Strength*. Let's begin!

Defining Your Theme

Focus! Your annual action plan theme is about setting your focus. It is a fun and interesting tool designed to focus your thoughts and actions on the most important things you want to accomplish in this planning cycle. When properly developed, your annual theme further compels you to action and keeps your thoughts positive and focused on the task(s) at hand.

To develop a theme for your Personal Annual Action Plan, review your prioritized lists created from your assessment (refer to page 225). What are the top three to five things you want to accomplish? Do you see a pattern or a common thread among them? Here are a few "theme" examples:

"The Year of Rejuvenation." This might apply to a year where you focus on revitalizing your body, mind, or career.

"The Year of Financial Success." This might apply to a year where your goals center on achieving a number of financial objectives.

"The Year of Great Relationships." This could apply to a year where the focus is on revitalizing, recreating, and renewing personal, family, or business relationships.

When writing your theme, there are no real rules except to keep it positive, lively, and fun. It should evoke emotion, a spark within you, and feel like it is PULLING you toward its achievement! This will likely take some practice and it's OK to begin with a theme that's "close" and tweak it along the way until you feel it's just right.

Take some time now to review your prioritized list and your list of things you need to *"start, continue and stop"* doing, and develop a theme for the year. Write this theme at the top of a new page (whether written electronically or on paper) entitled: "My Personal Annual Action Plan."

Setting Goals and Objectives

As you have learned, some people are intrinsically motivated by achievement, and goals and objectives are a natural part of their lives. In addition, their natural themes and talents may allow them to develop strengths in the area of achievement, goal setting, and getting things done. You likely know people who have this dynamic combination, or you may be one of them. They are the folks who say, *"I have never set a goal I did not meet."* For these people, setting and achieving goals simply feels easy and natural. They make lists of things to do and consistently and confidently tick them off as they accomplish each one, beaming with pride as they do.

For others, however, setting and achieving goals and objectives is not their thing and may actually be *de-*

Live from Strength

motivating because - to them - setting goals may evoke fear and symbolize failure. For some people, their intrinsic motivators, natural talents, and developed strengths, actually lead them away from setting goals and objectives, yet they are still capable of "achieving" great things. The problem is, as a society and as most "success" gurus will tell you – *"you must set goals and objectives in order to be successful."* Consequently, we continue to feel pressure to set goals even though many of us haven't been very good at it, have experienced mixed results, and likely have begun to devalue goal setting in general.

Whether you are naturally motivated to set and achieve goals and objectives or if they scare the heck out of you, or anywhere in between, this next section is for you.

Redefining Goals and Objectives

The first thing we are going to do is de-mystify goals and objectives and expose them for what they are – and what they are not.

Goals and objectives are simply one of many tools you can use to achieve your vision. As a tool, they need to be used appropriately and effectively, but only when they are needed. *It is important to understand that goals and objectives are not set in stone.* Goals can be changed, adapted and modified as needed and as we grow. It is OK to begin down a path toward an objective and then change direction because you discover that the objective is not right for you. Should you blindly continue toward a goal when you've discovered it is not in alignment with you just because you set that goal? Of course not! Or perhaps you find the goal beyond your reach, or you reach it more easily than you thought. Things change, and so will your goals.

Goals and objectives are simply milestones along your path to the life you desire. They are not hard and fast absolutes that, when not achieved, automatically equal failure.

One of the core principles we teach our clients is to re-define the word *failure*. We believe the only failure in life is the failure to define and live with intent, purpose and authenticity, the life you truly desire. If you have defined such a life and are doing your best to act with intent, purpose and authenticity, then whatever results you achieve is an added positive and simply cannot equate to failure. Oh, you may try a number of things and come up short on your journey, but those so-called "failures" are necessary steps to the eventual success that will be yours. For example, if you set a goal to double your current annual income from $50,000 to $100,000 and you only make $95,000 by the end of the year, have you really failed? We should all have such wonderful failures more often, don't you think? What can you do with an extra $45,000 that you didn't have before? Michael Eisner, former CEO of the Disney Company says it this way... *"Succeeding is not really a life experience that does that much good. Failing is a much more sobering and enlightening experience."* Failure is, very simply, a needed and important part of "success."

The point we are trying to make is this... You have now defined your life through your Personal Strategic Foundation; therefore, goals and objectives are simply *tools* for measuring and managing your progress toward your vision. Along the way you may not reach some of your goals and that's OK. You are striving toward them, with authenticity, purpose and intent, making progress, and you are already very, VERY successful! Remember, meaningful success comes from setting and pursuing goals in alignment with your Personal Strategic Foundation. To paraphrase Stephen Covey, *"If you are going to climb the ladder of success, make sure it is on the right wall."* Indeed!

Creating SMART Goals

When you set goals, you need to set them in a way that makes them effective for you. We like to use SMART[14] goals. SMART is an acronym for the following:

S – Specific

M – Measurable

A – Achievable

R – Relevant

T – Time-based

---

14 The acronym was first attributed to Doran, George T. "There's a S.M.A.R.T. way to write management's goals and objectives." Management Review, Nov 1981, Volume 70 Issue 11.

Let's take a look at each of these words in more detail:

- Goals need to be as *specific* as possible. The more specific, the more meaning it has to you and the more the goal draws you to it. Simply stating, "*Making more money,*" is not a goal and there is nothing there to pull you toward it. By stating, "*Making $100,000 this calendar year so I can take a dream vacation, afford a new BMW, buy those designer shoes from Italy, and better help families in need,*" is more specific and draws you to it from an emotional standpoint. Simply stating, "*Improving my health,*" is not a goal either, it is a desire. But stating, "*Improving my cardiovascular fitness by decreasing my time for running the mile by one minute, achieving 18% body fat, and reducing my waist measurement by two inches so I can look great at the beach this summer,*" is specific.

- By *measurable*, we mean you must be able to determine if you have achieved your goal and you need to be able to measure your progress. For example, you will know if you have made $100,000 in a given year or how much you have made to date. That's easy to measure. On the other hand, how do you measure the desire to be "in better health?" When do you know you are "more healthy?" Where did you start? How are you doing? How do you know when you have arrived?

- You must be able to actually *achieve* the goal. That is, the goal must be something you can reasonably expect to achieve within the time-frame set and under current circumstances. Setting a goal to make a million dollars this year when you have never made more than minimum wage is likely not achievable – yet (that is, without some extraordinary circumstances, such as a radical and successful new business idea or cashing in the winning lottery ticket, etc.). Setting goals that are impossible to achieve, regardless of how much you might desire the outcome, is ultimately not productive and they usually end up demeaning the goal process in the long run. Though we believe that not quite reaching a goal is not considered a failure, it is important to begin with goals that you can achieve, even if they are a bit of a stretch. This allows you to practice the process, experience positive results, and begin to build a good habit of achieving goals by continuously using them. This is especially important for those of us who are not naturally motivated by achievement.

- By *relevant*, we mean the goal must be in alignment with your Personal Strategic Foundation. Your Personal Strategic Foundation is your new reality and working toward any goal that is not in alignment with that foundation is simply no longer a valid use of your time.

- Goals need to have a completion *date or time*. Having a goal to reach a certain weight does not hold any meaning if there is not a time-frame involved. Once again, not achieving a goal within the time defined is not failure, however, simply saying you will achieve something and not setting a time to complete it allows you to continuously avoid the goal because there is no urgency for action. As far as timeframe, it is generally better to begin with shorter-term goals rather than longer-term goals so you can stay focused and rack up those feel good successes! If what you truly desire will take years to accomplish, then it is best to set shorter-term, intermediate goals on your path to achieving the longer-term objective.

At this point, it is time to develop at least one goal for each of the focus areas you prioritized during the Current State Assessment. For example, you might have an annual theme of "*The Year of Physical and Financial Fitness.*" Your three major focuses are getting healthy and fit physically, getting healthy and fit financially by building a savings account and paying off debt, and getting a new job that is more in line with your skill set and career objective that pays a higher annual salary. For this, you might create the following goals:

- By December 31, I will achieve physical fitness as I define it. I will weigh 185 lbs and will be able to run a mile in eight minutes.

- By July 31, I will obtain a new job in the field of engineering that pays an annual salary of $75,000 or more and provides me with career advancement and educational opportunities.

- By December 31, I will have saved $5,000 and have reduced my overall credit card debt to less than $2,000.

Each of these goals is very specific, time-based, achievable, and measurable. And since they are focused on your theme, they are definitely relevant.

Build an Action Plan for Each Goal

Once your goals are defined, it is time to build a plan of action for each one. A project plan, if you will. Let's take a look at how this works with the example goals from above.

Looking at the physical fitness objective, let's say you gave this a rating of 4 during your Current State Assessment. You go to the gym occasionally, but you know you need to *continue* and can go more consistently. You realize you need to *stop* eating junk food and drinking soda, and *start* eating a balanced diet and drinking more water. You also realize you need to add a cardio workout such as running or step aerobics at least twice a week and begin a disciplined weight training program.

Therefore, your action plan could look something what you see on the next page:

My Action Plan: Physically Fit by December 31:

- Join a weight loss support group, or find a mentor.
- Develop a nutrition plan.
- Clean out my cupboards and dump all unhealthy foods and beverages.
- Purchase healthy foods on a weekly basis.
- Develop a workout and weight training plan.
- Block out time in my calendar to go to the gym each week.
- Schedule runs on the weekends.

Of course, there are many other possible actions you could include such as going to the doctor for a physical check-up, hiring a personal trainer and nutritionist, taking a healthy cooking class, etc. The point is to get down on paper as many of the one-time and ongoing tasks and ideas needed for achieving this goal. If you are not sure where to begin in this process, you might find it helpful to work with someone (a mentor) who is also working toward the same goal, or has already achieved a similar goal and ask them what they are doing or what they did to get there.

Now turning your attention to the stated career goal, you might have rated yourself a 3 as you currently work as a construction laborer but you have always wanted to be an engineer. You don't have the education yet but you do have some experience that could get you an engineering assistant job, especially when they know of your long-term employability, and they may be willing to pay for part of your education.

An action plan for this goal may look something like what you see on the following page:

My Action Plan: New Career Position by July 31:

- Develop a list of my personal contacts (current and previous friends, family, teachers, co-workers, managers, etc.) in the industry or those who may know people in the industry.
- Develop a list of engineering firms in my area, i.e., my target firms, by talking to personal contacts and doing on-line and library research.
- Develop a list of engineering groups and associations where I could network with other engineers by talking with personal contacts and doing on-line and library research.
- Find contacts who know people in these firms through my personal network.
- Update my Facebook and LinkedIn profiles.
- Market myself through phone and email connections, or referrals to obtain "informational interviews" with my target firms.
- Get career and resume development guidance and coaching.
- Apply for entry level jobs, as applicable, with my target firms.
- Research the educational benefits provided by each.
- Research engineering colleges in the area and determine which have internship positions available with some of my targeted engineering firms.

Again, there are numerous actions one could take toward this goal, however, the intent is to brainstorm and list all of the possible actions you could take, sift through them, put them in order and build the action plan that works best for you.

Action Planning Tips

Action planning is a perfect time in the process to emphasize strengths vs. true inabilities. If you remember back when we showed you my unique themes of strengths, talent and abilities, you saw that I had a strength in "Taking Action." Thus, action planning is a natural skill of mine. It comes to me easily and it is easy for me to brainstorm, list and rank-order what needs to be done to get from point A to point B. I have never known a time when I could not "navigate" a project plan.

Action planning may, however, be a true inability (something for which one does NOT have natural talent) for others. Thus, I am providing the following tips as I recognize that what may be easy and intuitive to me, may not be so to others:

- Action planning can be done both forwards and backwards and different people find one or the other more effective.

- To look at it from a *forward* perspective, ask yourself, *"What is the first thing I need to do?"* Then, *"what is next?"* And so on until you have listed the very last thing before the goal is reached. You, in essence, build the plan moving forward, one step at a time.

- To look at it from a *backward perspective*, envision that you are already at your goal. Now ask yourself, *"What was the last thing I must have done to get here?"* Then from there, you step back and ask again, *"What was the last thing I must have done to get here?,"* and so on until you get back to your current state.

- Start by brainstorming "actions" (what needs to be done) and don't worry about the order of the actions. Once you have all your ideas out, then review them to see where the sequence of steps may be. Gaps will show and you can fill them in.

- Mind mapping, a visual brainstorming technique, helps visual learners express the actions needed to achieve goals. Check Wikipedia for information and resources on this technique.

- Kinesthetic learners may be able to better order the action items by writing them on note cards or sticky notes and manipulating them as needed. Any missing steps will become readily apparent. This is also a good technique for all of us to use to rank-order action steps.

- It is very difficult, even for practiced planners, to see more than a few months ahead, so it is OK if your action steps feel a little fuzzy, uncertain, and subject to change beyond three months. Adjust as you get closer.

- If it is not your strength, it is OK to ask for help. Remember, one of the principles of the one who *Lives from Strength* is to let go of the need to do things that are not in alignment with their gifts. So seek assistance and ask for help!

Once you have worked through your list and created your goals and action plans, add them to the Personal Annual Action Plan document that you began when you developed your theme for the year. Keep a copy of your plan with you at all times, or certainly in a place where you can access it readily each week as you develop your Weekly Accomplishments Lists.

Weekly Accomplishments Lists

So far, you have developed a theme and goals to focus your actions on the major things you wish to accomplish this planning cycle (this year). Now you will begin to focus your attention on narrowing these longer-term goals into near-term *ACTIONS*.

Begin with developing a weekly "to do" list of actions and objectives you can accomplish within the week. Why weekly lists? As mentioned earlier in this chapter, one week provides enough time to schedule your time and accomplish significant chunks of activities, but short enough to effectively control the time without fear of significant changes in your schedule. A monthly accomplishment plan is an alternative and if it works better for you, that's OK too. Or even a combination of the two. What is important is the act of translating the annual action plan into manageable and achievable activities that need to be done "right now" and doing it in a way that works best for you.

A Weekly Accomplishments List is a simple list of activities or actions you will complete or accomplish in the upcoming week. Once again, they are prioritized by your theme and goals, but may include actions that move you toward other things in your Personal Strategic Foundation. Your list may even include some of the routine and mundane things you must do each week, such as: Clean the house, pay your bills, do the laundry, etc.

A Weekly Accomplishments List also includes scheduling time for yourself in your weekly calendar. As in our examples, if one of your goals is getting healthy, then you will block out time for exercise. If you desire to write a book, you will block out time to write. If you want to focus on developing relationships with family or your significant other, you will schedule that time as well.

Once an item on your list is complete, you cross it off your list. If you have done all you can to move an item forward during that week but were unable to complete it, simply carry it over to next week's list until it's done and you can cross it off your list.

We recommend you develop your weekly list each Sunday evening before going to bed. This will give your subconscious mind the opportunity to work on these items overnight. It will also give you confidence knowing that you have a plan for tomorrow. You will likely sleep better as well and will actually start looking forward to "getting started" in the morning! Alternatively, you might develop your Weekly Accomplishments List first thing Monday morning before digging into work, if that works best for you. Either way, these plans give you the direction and focus for this week's activities that are in alignment with your Personal Strategic Foundation, which will keep you moving toward the life of your dreams!

Weekly Accomplishments Lists are more than simple lists of things to do. They *ARE* the activity planning tool for turning the dreams and desires of your Personal Strategic Foundation into disciplined action, and your prioritized activities within your theme and goals into scheduled commitments. The very act of developing the list is as powerful and important as the lists themselves. This planning activity keeps your vision, mission, and values front and center and focuses your activity and schedule on what is truly important to you so you can get where you want to go!

Example of a Weekly Accomplishments List

A Weekly Accomplishments List may look like the following for someone who has the goals we defined earlier on page 250.

My Accomplishment List - Week of: January 15th
Fitness:
- Monday - Run 4 miles at lunch
- Tuesday - Lift weights at lunch
- Wednesday - 7:00 AM Yoga class
- Thursday - Walk with wife after work
- Friday - Run 4 miles at lunch
- Saturday – AM Basketball game with the guys
- Sunday – REST!

New Career Position:
- Research list of colleges that have engineering programs.
- Research list of local engineering groups and associations.
- Attend networking event at local chamber of commerce on Wednesday evening.
- Attend career fair at the technical college Saturday afternoon.

Savings and Debt Reduction:
- Review budget against actual spending for past six months.
- Sign up at work for automatic deduction of $50 per pay check into savings.

Develop a Weekly Accomplishments List

To develop your Weekly Accomplishment List, review your theme and the action plans for your three to five goals for the year, and ask yourself, *"What activities need to be done THIS WEEK to move me closer to my goals?"* Next, review your vision, mission, and values, in total, and determine if there are other action items that need to be added to the list. Now review your household and work actions that need to be done and put them on the list.

Once the list is complete, group them in prioritized order in sections such as "personal," "work," "home," etc. Now schedule your time to complete these items in your calendar. Block out sufficient time and make a personal appointment with yourself, especially for those items related to your theme.

Scheduling is important as it creates the time needed to "do" the actions that help you live each day in alignment with your true self! Commit time to those activities you have defined as truly important to you, and then follow through! All of the work you have done to this point is valuable and the dreams you have defined are worthy of action to make them your new reality.

Daily Action Plans

Action can only be taken in the moment – right now. Thus, the most important plan is the plan for today! Your Personal Annual Action Plan sets the overall theme and goals while your Weekly Accomplishments List sets the objectives for the week. Now it's time to translate the annual and weekly plans into your Daily Action Plan.

Your Daily Action Plan is simply a list of the six most important things you need to do today, listed and prioritized in order of importance. You develop this list from your Weekly Accomplishments List.

This simple technique comes from Ivy Lee who gave this idea to the executives at Bethlehem Steel at the turn of the last century. The story goes something like this...

Charles Schwab, then president of Bethlehem Steel, asked Mr. Lee, a well known efficiency expert at the time, to help improve efficiencies at the plant. Mr. Lee said he could do that if he could spend 15 minutes with Mr. Schwab's executives. *"How much will this cost?"* Schwab asked. Mr. Lee said, *"Nothing, unless it works. After three months, you can send me a check for whatever you feel it's worth to you."*

Mr. Lee did what he said and spent 15 minutes with Mr. Schwab's executive staff. The executives used Mr. Lee's plan, listing the six most important things they had to do each day and working them in order of priority. At the end of three months, Mr. Schwab sent Mr. Lee a check for $35,000! Now consider what $35,000 would be worth in today's dollars, over 100 years later! This is the extraordinary power of this simple tool. And now, after developing a clear and compelling Personal Annual Action Plan, you already know what your most important tasks are as you have defined them, making this tool even more powerful as you act, each day, in alignment with your Personal Strategic Foundation.

Develop Your Daily Action Plan

To develop your Daily Action Plan, review your Weekly Accomplishments List and select the six most important things you need to do TODAY to move toward your goals. Write down each one and prioritize the action items based on how you have prioritized your Personal Annual Action Plan. Now begin working from the top of your list. Work the first one until you can go no further or until it is completed. Then start on number two. Rinse and repeat! Sound simple? GOOD! *Simple* works; and simple is why this one simple idea is one of the most valuable and powerful personal growth tools available, as Charles Schwab found out for himself!

We recommend that you create this list at the end of each day for the next day, for two reasons. First, as mentioned before, your subconscious mind will work on these items during the night. You will wake with new and fresh ideas for getting things done, and you will likely find you have "ah ha" moments in your morning shower more frequently. Second, by writing these things down before going to bed, your mind will be at ease, and you will sleep better knowing you have your plan in place for tomorrow.

Execute on your Daily Action Plan by simply starting your day working on the first item on your list. You work it until you can't work it any longer, or until you complete it, and then you begin to work on number two. You continue in this manner for the remainder of the day until the day is done. It is OK if you have items remaining on your list. What is important is that you focus on THE most important thing you need to do until you can no longer focus on it. Ask yourself this question, *"What other method is there to ensure complete focus on the most important things I need to do to move my life forward?"* We have not found one. This is simple and highly effective *(because it is so simple)*.

Remember, you can break your list into "work" and "personal," or you can combine the two. Whatever works best for you IS what is best. Oh, and don't forget, one of those six most important things may be something like "rest," "fun," "exercise," "connect with my spouse," "attend my kid's soccer game," etc. A life where you *Live from Strength* means that work, life, and love are all lived with the intent, purpose and authenticity you have defined in your Personal Strategic Foundation.

The Power of Positive Affirmations

Affirmations are positive statements expressed to "affirm" what you really want, and they support the way you are choosing to live your life. They are the positive little things you say to yourself to build confidence, affirm your beliefs, and change your thoughts and attitudes. Creating positive affirmations that resonate with you is one of the most important steps in this entire process.

All of us today whether we are conscious of it or not, use affirmations. The problem is that many of us have a number of highly destructive thought patterns, or negative affirmations. Pay attention to how you feel as you read through the next few sentences. You may even identify with some of these more common "self talk" thoughts.

Have you ever said to yourself, *"I'm so fat!"* Or, *"I'm so ugly"* Or when we mess up, we might say, *"I'm so stupid! I can't get anything right?"* How did reading these words make you feel? Likely not very good. Each time we say things like this to ourselves, we "affirm" our weight problem, our weaknesses, or our fears and in effect, we end up focusing on the exact thing we don't want.

Louise Hay, a pioneer in the use of positive affirmations in her ground-breaking book, *You Can Heal Your Life*, asks the question, *"Would you talk to a three-year old the way you talk to yourself?"* Would you really say, *"Gross! You're so fat!"* to a child? Of course not!

Would you allow a friend, relative, or co-worker to talk to you that way? As a rational and fully functioning adult, you know that type of talk to be abusive behavior and you would not tolerate it.

So why then, do we think it's OK to talk to ourselves that way? Is it any less destructive or abusive? It may, in fact, be even more hurtful because we are more likely to believe it when we say it to ourselves. It's not appropriate, it's damaging and unloving, and it's time to let it go. Simply replace each negative with a positive – and soon, you won't hear that negative self talk anymore.

The Personal Annual Action Plan includes using personalized daily *positive* affirmations to help you make the mental and emotional changes necessary so you can become the person you are meant to be and live the life of your dreams. Your positive affirmations are specific to you and need to be repeated at least daily in a way that works best for you. It could be once each morning, once each evening, both, or even more frequently during the day.

Positive affirmations are part of your Daily Action Plan to help you achieve your vision. These affirmations work with you to manifest your life of direction, purpose and integrity on a daily basis. Positive affirmations not only affirm those things we desire, but they also harness the power of the Law of Attraction.

The Law of Attraction

The Law of Attraction simply stated is: *"You become what you think about most"* and was the subject of the extraordinary book and movie we mentioned earlier, *The Secret*, by Rhonda Byrne. The book and movie are a collection of anecdotes and stories regarding the power of positive thought from many of the top thinkers in the area of personal growth. That IS the secret - you *can* attract and become that which you think about most. Henry Ford said it this way... *"Whether you think that you can, or that you can't, you are usually right."*

This can be a good thing or, unfortunately, there is a counter opposite. That is, if you continually think about positive, affirming things, what you truly desire while having a strong belief in yourself, then you will attract the positive things you desire. If, however, you continue to repeat negative thoughts of fear and failure, visioning bad things happening to you, or convincing yourself that you are simply not lucky in life, etc., *that* is exactly what you will attract into your life. The more positive the thoughts, the more positive the results, and vice versa.

Now, this idea carries with it some fairly heavy accountability. If you look around your life and you see love, joy, happiness, wealth, abundance, health, excitement, etc., you have likely done a good job of attracting those things to you by your positive thought patterns, attitudes, and actions.

But the opposite is also true. If you look around and find unhappiness, misery, poverty, scarcity, disease, and boredom, you have likely attracted those things to you as well. Though bad things may happen to good people sometimes, regardless of their thought patterns, the bottom line is - whatever you have in your life is, to a large extent, a result of what you have attracted to yourself through your own thought patterns, attitudes, and actions (which include in-actions).

Knowing this brings about the next great "challenge" for you in defining and living from strength. The challenge to accept your circumstances for what they are and deciding, right here and now, to change any negative circumstances for the better by practicing positive thoughts, attitudes, and beliefs until the positive actions become second nature - and becomes your new of way being.

The POWER of your Personal Strategic Foundation is that you now have the structure on which to begin the process of thinking daily about what you really want, so you can attract it! It provides a vision of the life you desire and shows you the value you provide to the world so the world can give back to you in abundance, and it includes a set of values to which you live your life. The process of assessing where you are relative to your foundation has provided you with ideas on some of the negative thoughts and actions you will change so you can manifest your dreams. And you have built goals and objectives to focus on those things most important to you at this moment.

Positive affirmations, repeated at least daily, are a powerful additional tool for overcoming negative thoughts and actions, replacing negative mental tapes with a new set of positive tapes that tell you who you *really* are, how successful you are, and that you have the love, joy, excitement, wealth, health, abundance, friendships, etc., that you truly desire.

As with any change, it will take some time before the positive thoughts, ideas and attitudes take hold and completely "replace" the negative ones. This replacement process usually goes something like this... You see yourself in the mirror and immediately have your standard negative thought, *"Man, I am fat!"* Now that you have focused your life on your strengths and identified your negative thoughts, feelings and beliefs that are getting in your way, you may recognize, AFTER you say this to yourself, that saying this was wrong. Because you have developed your positive affirmations, however, you can now stop, look at yourself again and say, *"I am fit, trim and cut and I look GOOD!"*

The point here is that you need three things to make the change. First, you need *awareness* that a particular thought or attitude NEEDS to change. Second, you need to have the "counter-positive" replacement statement already thought out ahead of time. Finally, you need to practice saying the affirmation(s) and practice awareness IN THE

MOMENT to recognize the opportunity to replace the negative thought when it happens. Thus, over time, you will begin to recognize the very moment where you would normally say something negative and will immediately replace it with the positive one, before the other is even spoken.

But "thinking" about something is only the first step in the process. Once you have created your written list of positive affirmations, it's time to *ACT!* Your plan of action comes in the form of a Personal Annual Action Plan, Weekly Accomplishments Lists, Daily Action Plans, and reading and repeating, with purpose and intent, your daily affirmations.

Now it's time to develop the positive affirmations that will resonate with and work for you.

How to Create Positive Affirmations

One of the best tools we have found for turning around "true weaknesses" (negative thoughts, attitudes and beliefs) is to create positive affirmations to "reprogram" your thoughts, attitudes and beliefs so they are more in line with your choice to *Live from Strength*. To do this, however, you need to both discover the "counter-positive" thought, attitude and belief and then believe it.

Bryon Katie outlines in her book, *Loving What Is: How Four Questions Can Change Your Life,* a great method to help you turn around negative thought patterns/processes into positive believes, and it goes something like this...

- First, take a thought, attitude or belief you believe is holding you back. Remember the list you created to identify those things you need to STOP doing in your assessment? That's a good place to find them. These are often negative thoughts and attitudes you simply need to turn around. Let's say your negative thought is: *"I am not very confident in my abilities."* That is, for example you may have discovered during the assessment that you needed to stop letting your lack of confidence get in the way of living a certain aspect of your vision or values.

- So the first question you ask is, *"Is it true?"* In this case you might answer, *"Well, it sure feels true, especially when I am under pressure or out of my comfort zone."* So the result is generally, a qualified maybe. That is, for most thoughts, attitudes and beliefs, there is a shred of truth that is based, generally, on past experience or in isolated situations. But we have already learned that the past has no bearing on the future, unless we allow it to, right? Of course!

- Thus, the second question to ask is, *"Is it UNIVERSALLY true?"* That is, is it always true, in all circumstances and always true in the great scheme of universal laws? Here, there are likely things you are extremely confident about. Perhaps in some knowledge, skill or ability. That is, where you are practiced, you are confident. Thus, we generally find that our negative thoughts, attitudes and beliefs do not hold up when truly put to the test of universal truth.

- Now, the third question becomes, *"What would your life look like if you were always confident?"* This question is about envisioning your life in the "counter-positive." What would your life look like, feel like, be like, if you faced each situation, every day, with confidence? Attempt to paint this picture, truly envision a life of confident, purposeful action!

- Finally, the fourth question is, *"What is a positive expression of that life?"* In this example, it is "what is a positive expression of a life lived with confidence?" You now begin to draft a statement such as, *"I live and act with confidence every day!"* Or, *"I face the challenges of the day confident in my ability to overcome all obstacles."*

This process can be used on any negative thought, attitude or belief and it almost always yields a powerful and compelling counter-positive statement that, when repeated as a daily affirmation, can, over time, give you the power to reprogram your negative thoughts, attitudes and beliefs, and to let them go, FOREVER!

Develop Your Daily Affirmations

To develop your daily affirmations:

- Create a list and title it something like, "My Personal Affirmations."

- Review your vision and values statements to select from them some of the necessary attitudes and beliefs you will need – already written AS affirmations – and add them to your affirmations list.

  For example, your vision may have a statement such as… "I am prosperous and the world provides an abundance of wealth and resources for my every need." Or, you might have a value of, "I am kind, considerate, and respectful of others." Remember, we suggested you write your vision and values as positive affirming statements. We did this for a reason! Because, when written this way, they naturally become your positive affirmations.

- Referring to your Personal Annual Action Plan, review your Current State Assessment and your major goals and theme for the year and ask yourself what positive beliefs and thoughts are needed to turn your assessment values into a 9 or 10, to reach your goals and live your theme for the year? Add these positive beliefs and thoughts to your affirmations list.

  For example, in your vision you see yourself with wealth yet you ranked it a 5 because you are doing well, but you want to do even better. In this case, you may need to focus more on gratitude while developing a belief of "abundance."

Or perhaps you have a fitness goal and some of the things you said you needed to "stop" doing was eating fast food, and "start" believing that you eat only wholesome natural foods. In this case, you may need to develop a belief that you ARE fit and healthy and you fuel your body with foods that are good for you.

And if your theme for the year is to develop healthier relationships with your loved ones and friends, you may need to develop a belief that your relationships are healthy, positive and supportive.

- Review your prioritization exercises and select from the items you would like to change in your life for this year's Personal Annual Action Plan and add any additional necessary thoughts and attitudes to your positive affirmations list.

For example, in your current Personal Annual Action Plan, you might have prioritized having more open and honest communications as one of the top things you need to improve. Perhaps, in the past, you may have shied away from being direct because you thought it too confrontational but you always believed honesty is the best policy. Thus, you would want to develop an attitude of openness and directness while continuing to honor your positive thoughts of honesty as the best policy and include this as one of your written positive affirmations.

- Finally, review the list of "true weaknesses" you developed back on page 138; your list of negative thoughts, attitudes and beliefs you saw as true weaknesses. List these items in your document.

- Review each item on the list and as needed, create a counter positive affirmation, a positive statement written in the present tense *as if you have already achieved the goal* or you are already living the value. For those negative thoughts, attitudes and beliefs, use the process defined above to create the affirmation, and the belief that it is possible.

For example, if you desire wealth and financial abundance in your vision, you might craft an affirmation such as: "I have an abundance of financial wealth, the peace of mind that comes with financial freedom, and I am truly grateful."

For a fitness or health goal, you might affirm: "I am healthy and fit and I am at my ideal weight. I look and feel great!"

To develop better family relationships, an affirmation may be: "I have happy and healthy relationships with my siblings and their families. Our time together is warm, friendly and relaxed."

And to develop open and honest communication, your affirmation may be: "I am open, clear and direct in my communications and believe honesty is the best policy."

- To use your affirmations, read them at least once each day. A good time to read them is at the same time you develop your Daily Action Plan. Other good times for review are just before bedtime and right after you wake up in the morning.

Affirmation Do's!

When developing your positive affirmations:

- Do use the present tense such as "I have," "I am," "We are," "It is," etc. Your mind and the universe will begin to believe you already have these things and your thoughts will begin to attract them. Watch out for modifiers or phrases such as, "I will have," "I will be," "I would like to," "it could be," "I intend to," etc. Your mind and the universe will hear the "doubt" in these statements and you will be *forever* "acquiring" rather than "having" or "being."

- Do craft *positive* affirmations that focus on what you want. Watch out for affirmations that negate the things you don't want such as "eliminate stress," "get rid of fat," "get out of debt," etc. Your mind and the universe will hear only the words "stress," "fat," and "debt" and that is what you will continue to attract.

- Do use positive statements and words such as health, wealth, freedom, fun, love, peace of mind, and words that make you feel good. Your mind and the universe will then focus only on these positive aspects of your life.

- Do make your affirmations short and to the point. If they are more than two lines, they are too long. Focus on the key words that are important and use only enough words to convey the message and make the affirmation readable.

- Do remember your affirmations can be adjusted. They can and will morph and adapt to your needs as you grow and change.

- Do modify your affirmations periodically as you get better at understanding what words most motivate and inspire you.

Reviewing the POWER of Action

Your Personal Annual Action Plan gives you POWER! The POWER of *focused*, *purposeful* and *intentional* action, each and every day that is in alignment with your Personal Strategic Foundation. The result is LIVING, not just dreaming about the life you truly desire; a life with a clear direction (vision), a meaningful purpose (mission), and one that is in alignment with your authentic self (values).

By focusing on a theme for the year, based on an honest and prioritized assessment of where you are, your daily actions are honed in on what is truly important to you, right now. Through goals and their corresponding action plans, your actions are now purposeful and your progress can be effectively measured. Through Weekly Accomplishments Lists, Daily Action Plans, and Positive Affirmations, you are acting with intent, each and every day, to live and create what you desire most in your life.

Use your Personal Annual Action Plan to create the daily guidance needed to act, with confidence, purpose and intent, to truly fulfill the promise of your Personal Strategic Foundation as you *Live from Strength*. Now it is up to you to put your plan into action... one year, one week, one day, and one step at a time! You CAN do it!

Keeping It Fresh

"Living involves tearing up one rough draft after another."
Unknown

"Every day you may make progress. Every step may be fruitful. Yet there will stretch out before you an ever-lengthening, ever-ascending, ever-improving path. You know you will never get to the end of the journey. But this, so far from discouraging, only adds to the joy and glory of the climb."
Winston Churchill

One of the most important concepts of living from strength is in understanding the concept of *becoming*. A life well lived is not about a destination, the end result, but the process of *becoming* the person you choose to be by continually modifying and adapting your Personal Strategic Foundation as you learn and grow on your journey.

Quoting Earl Nightingale once again, *"Success is the progressive realization of a worthwhile goal."* That is, success IS the journey, not just the destination. You are successful BECAUSE you are working toward something you consider worthwhile, not just when you achieve it.

This means it is perfectly OK to change your mind about your direction (vision), purpose (mission), and values (ethics), as you progress on your journey and as your life circumstances change. But this does not mean you will blow willy-nilly with the wind in all directions, making radical course changes. With a well-crafted Personal Annual Action Plan based on your Personal Strategic Foundation, you will find the changes you make are more like minor mid-course corrections that will continually confirm your essential foundation. But things do change and it is important to plan time to take these things into account and adapt your plan.

Additionally, as we go through our daily life, we occasionally lose track of where we are heading and start to feel a bit off center. Reviewing your Personal Strategic Foundation and Personal Annual Action Plan at this time can be very valuable and will help you get back on track quickly.

Because you are alive and ever changing, your Personal Annual Action Plan must be a living tool as well. It is important to maintain and update your plan as your life changes on your journey.

A maintenance and update plan includes:

- An *annual comprehensive review* and update of your Personal Annual Action Plan, including:

  - Review and revision of your Personal Strategic Foundation.

- An honest re-assessment of where you are *currently* toward living your Personal Strategic Foundation.

- Review and revise your Personal Annual Action Plan including new and revised goals and action plans for the upcoming year.

• *Periodic status reviews* with minor adjustments and changes, as needed, between each annual comprehensive review.

• *As-needed re-assessments*, especially whenever you start to feel "a little off" and out of alignment.

Performing an Annual Plan Review

We recommend reviewing your Personal Annual Action Plan once each year (which, of course, makes perfect sense since this is an annual plan). This is accomplished by simply walking through the components of your plan, including the Personal Strategic Foundation, making any necessary adjustments or changes, and re-focusing your efforts to the new theme, goals and/or action plans developed for the new year.

Doing this review and update at the end of each calendar year as you start the New Year is a good habit to develop. Many of us have a few days off during the holidays, so setting aside quiet time to reflect and review during this period works well. Even if you are one who must work through the holidays, the New Year - with its hope of renewal, reinvention, rejuvenation, and rebirth - is a perfect time to re-evaluate your plan and refocus on living the life you truly desire. And the icing on the cake is that NOW, your "New Year's Resolutions" will have real meaning to you because they are based on a solid foundation that you created. You will find them motivating and easier to work toward.

The periodic review process is as follows:

- Review your Personal Strategic Foundation:

  - Review and revise your Personal Vision. Make some quiet time to review what you have written, look at your vision board, and re-evaluate other tools you use to define the person and life you are becoming and the life you want to live. Ask yourself what has changed in your life that impacts this vision. Does anything no longer feel right to you? If so, how or why? Any additions? What are they? Have you achieved some of the things in your vision and need to create new challenges? Or are these items constants in your life and thus you simply need to maintain them? Reset a new date, three to five years in the future, for your vision. Revise your written vision documents and your vision board as needed.

  - Review and revise your Personal Mission Statement. Do you believe what is stated is still how you create value in your world? Have you honed or clarified your unique purpose through intentional use of your unique gifts? Have you clarified what you do in any way through your recent experience? Revise your Personal Mission Statement as needed.

– Review and revise your values. Have you been able to honor all of them? If not, why not? Does this indicate you have not focused appropriately on them? Or, rather, is that particular value really not that important to you and you need to delete or revise it? Revise and adjust as needed.

• Revise and update your Personal Profile:

– Revise the descriptions of your strengths and hone how you use them in a positive way and how you have come to realize the impact of your strengths taken to extreme.

– Revise the description of your learning style(s) and how you uniquely communicate and process information. How can you communicate more effectively and how can you more effectively use your gifts for better communication.

– Revise the descriptions of your natural motivations style and hone how this impacts you to take positive action and note when things "de-motivate" you.

- Repeat the Current State Assessment by:

  - Evaluating each statement in your revised vision, mission, and values from 1 to 10 as to whether you have attained or are living them day-to-day.

  - For those receiving an 8 or less, ask yourself what you need to *start*, *stop*, and *continue* doing to acquire what you want, or to move your life in this direction.

  - Take time to note your accomplishments and positive changes in your assessment scores, regardless of how large or small, and make a note of just how far you have come.

- Reprioritize your findings based on importance, urgency, and order and select your new top three to five priority areas of focus.

- Create a new Personal Annual Action Plan based on your prioritized areas of focus, including:

  - A new theme for the year.

  - A new or modified set of goals.

  - A new action plan for each goal.

  - A new or revised set of positive affirmations.

- Work the new plan.

  - Make Weekly Accomplishments Lists based on the new theme and goals.

- Read your affirmations daily.

- Plan your day by creating your Daily Action Plan listing the six most important things you need to do.

- Act on your Daily Action Plan with purpose and intent.

• *Take time to celebrate your accomplishments and make time to practice feeling gratitude.* These things are very important to sustaining your progress. If you have been working the plan, you have likely achieved a great deal this past year! Review the list you created above and congratulate, TRULY CONGRATULATE yourself for all you have done! Even if your accomplishment list seems small to you, remember that by using this process you have likely accomplished far more than you would have before. ANY movement in the direction toward living the life you truly desire is a wonderful achievement! GOOD FOR YOU!

Periodic Progress Reviews

Progress on your life journey comes in small steps, not usually in leaps and bounds, making it important to periodically review your progress toward your goals and toward becoming more aligned to your Personal Strategic Foundation. We recommend at least a quarterly review, although a monthly review is often better. It really depends on the types of goals you have set for yourself and how frequently you need to assess your progress.

To go through the periodic progress review you need to:

- Review your progress toward each of the major goals you defined. Are you on track? If so, what will you do to maintain this momentum? If not, what do you need to "start, stop, and continue" doing to get back on track? Do you need to modify the goal? If so, that is OK! Adjust as needed.

- Review and revise your personal affirmations and align them to any changes you may have made in your progress review above.

- Work the revised plan using Weekly Accomplishments Lists, Daily Action Plans, and by reading your positive affirmations daily.

- Recognize and celebrate your accomplishments and practice feeling gratitude for all that you have done. List those accomplishments, even the little ones! Celebrate even the smallest of things where you have lived in alignment to your Personal Strategic Foundation. Remember this is a process of *becoming* and aligning to your authentic self. You are experiencing little successes every day as you create and live the life of your dreams, so celebrate them as you go!

Live from Strength

What To Do When You Feel Off Course

One of the most powerful tools presented in this book is the *Current State Assessment*. This tool can be used at any time to help you re-align yourself to your Personal Strategic Foundation.

When you feel off or un-centered, it is usually a result of not living up to one or more of your values in your Personal Strategic Foundation. You might also be feeling off-center because you are not focusing on your mission, or not moving your life in the direction you had set for yourself. Or, you may have had life changes that impact your foundation in a relatively profound way and it's time to adjust the plan to meet the new reality.

Therefore, whenever you feel a bit off and feel the need to re-center, we recommend that you repeat the *Current State Assessment*, as follows:

- For each statement in the Personal Strategic Foundation, rate them from 1 to 10, with 10 being – *"You have it now, or you are already living it every day."*

- Review your Personal Profile to see where you can better align yourself to your unique gifts. Are you falling back on old habits and ways of doing things or are you intentionally applying your unique gifts to the challenges in your life?

- Compare these results to prior assessments (this is one reason we suggested keeping and versioning all your planning documents). Do you see areas where your results have changed for the worse? If so, these are likely areas indicating a loss of focus.

- For those items with an 8 or less, once again ask yourself what you need to "start, stop, or continue" doing.

- Compare these results to prior assessments. Have you truly stopped doing those things identified? Have you begun doing the things you need to start? Have you continued those things you were already doing well?

The results from your review should give you insight into why you are feeling off or un-centered. Typically, our clients report that within 15 minutes they can identify the problem, make a quick adjustment, and feel back on track. They easily discovered where they had strayed and because they were armed with the tools and information needed to regain their focus and get back on track, they could do so quickly.

But if repeating the Current State Assessment does not help you, the likely cause could be that there is something that needs to change in your Personal Strategic Foundation (vision, mission or values). If so, review your Personal Strategic Foundation and look for areas where you feel change is needed. If you make adjustments, review and revise your goals and action plans accordingly.

Final Thoughts

After completing *The Personal Growth Challenge*™ process defined in this book, you now have developed the components for success, as you have defined it for yourself, that will stand the test of time: a clear strategy, an honest assessment of your current state, and a plan of focused action to get you where you want to go. Your strategy, or Personal Strategic Foundation, comes from a compelling *vision* that creates direction for your life, a *mission* that focuses your actions and provides meaning and purpose, and a set of *values* that guides your daily decisions and defines your authentic self. You know where to begin because you honestly and effectively evaluated your *current state*. The focused actions that will lead you to your vision are clearly defined in your Personal Annual Action Plan. Your plan sets your goals based on what is most important to you right now and then drives your action down to the most important things you need to do today; because, in the end, today, this moment, is all we can control and manage to effect change and growth! And your values will empower you to act and make decisions each day, with confidence and authenticity, knowing you are living with integrity while focusing your activities on those things that will most likely lead you to success, as you have defined it. As a result, you are likely feeling more fulfilled, having more fun and finding more time for fun and fulfilling activities than ever before! And you are probably experiencing deeper, more meaningful relationships.

Your daily focus takes any worry out of the "change equation." To manage change, you need only think about the decision right in front of you, right now, and ask yourself whether this opportunity is in alignment with your Personal Strategic Foundation, and if it is not, discard it and move on. And since you are acting with intention, purpose and authenticity to achieve your dreams, you already ARE successful. There may be setbacks along the way, but if you stay in alignment with your authentic self, your STRENGTHS, and continue to act with purpose and intent, not only will you get where you intend to go, but personal fulfillment and success are yours already!

You now understand that you have powerful and valuable natural gifts that define your unique purpose and your true mission here on Earth. Using your unique gifts, you can provide real value to those you serve, feel valued for what you do, and feel fulfillment in the doing. By continually delivering that value the world (and the universe) will give back to you in abundance and in proportion to the value you provide, so that you may live a prosperous life and provide for yourself and your family.

Your unique gifts, as defined in your Personal Profile, are a tool for you to use to solve any challenge, overcome any obstacle, and reach any milestone, and they represent the acorn of your very success. When well tended, fertilized and watered, this acorn will grow into a mighty, solid oak tree with unlimited growth potential! And you now understand that these strengths, when taken to extreme can also be the weaknesses others perceive in you. The end result, however, whether you are talking about a drive to success or overcoming a weakness, only a focus on your strengths, your unique gifts, is an effort worthy of your time and attention! Thus, to *Live from Strength* is a positive, affirming and uplifting view of life and a powerful way of living!

Remember, *The Personal Growth Challenge*™ is not a static process. You are constantly changing and growing. So it is necessary to consistently and periodically review and revise your personal plan, just like a successful business during their annual strategic planning meetings. The bottom line, *The Personal Growth Challenge*™ *is both a process for defining "a life well lived" - as well as "a life-long process for living well."* These are powerful tools used to define, create, and manage the life you desire, combined with a set of attitudes and thought patterns that can give your life true meaning, purpose, joy, consistency, and fulfillment each and every day, as you *Live from Strength*!

We sincerely hope you are now enjoying the benefits of a clear strategy and focused action. You may find that even after defining your Personal Strategic Foundation and executing your Personal Annual Action Plan that obstacles remain in your path to the life you truly desire. The concepts and tools in *Live from Strength* are not a cure-all, but what this process does do is it helps you overcome any fear and anxiety that may stem from not being in touch with your authentic self. By creating a clear direction, purpose and sense of integrity in your life, most of those anxieties simply fall away.

If, however, you continue to experience emotional issues that you feel are holding you back, you may need the help of a professional, such as a counselor, therapist, or psychologist. We highly recommend you seek out the help you need if that is the case. It is our hope and experience, however, that by having a clear strategic foundation and plan in place for your life, you will now have the information to first recognize and better understand how any personal issue you face impacts your life and personal growth. The result of *The Personal Growth Challenge*™ process is the power and confidence to take positive action to solve or mitigate the effects of such issues, whether you tackle them yourself or with the aid of a professional. Either way, you are in control.

Other Resources

In addition, we highly recommend the following resources for deepening your understanding and utilization of some of the tools and techniques we have discussed in this book.

- **Using Affirmations:** To find out more about the power and use of positive affirmations, we highly recommend:

  - *You Can Heal Your Life*, Louise L. Hay, Hay House, Gift Edition, 1999.

- **Understanding the Universal Law of Attraction:** To find out more about "the secret" and using the universal law of attraction in your life, we recommend:

  - *The Secret*, Rhonda Byrne, Atria Books, 2006

  - *Law of Attraction*: The Science of Attracting More of What You Want and Less of What You Don't, Michael J. Losier, Wellness Center, 2007

- **Understanding Your Strengths:** To find out more about your personal strengths and to take the Clifton StrengthsFinder® test, we recommend:

  - *Strengths Finder 2.0*: Tom Rath, Gallup Press, 2007

  - www.strengthsfinder.com, the Gallop organization's StrengthsFinder® Website.

- **Understanding the Laws of Success:** To find out more about the great laws of success and to discover which will work best for you, we recommend:

  - *Think and Grow Rich*, Napoleon Hill, Create Space, 2010 (updated from original).

  - The 7 Habits of Highly Effective People, Stephen R. Covey, Free Press, 2003.

  - *The Success Principles*: Jack Canfield, Harper Paper Backs, 2006.

  - *Live Your Best Life*; A Treasury of Wisdom, Wit, Advice, Interviews, and Inspiration from O, The Oprah Magazine, Oxmoor House, 2005.

  - Living Deeply: *The Art and Science of Transformation in Everyday Life,* Schlitz, Vieten & Amorok, IONS/New Harbinger, 2007.

- **Living a Principle-Centered Life:** To find out more about living to your values and principles, we highly recommend:

  - *Principle-Centered Leadership*, Steven R. Covey, Simon & Schuster, 1991.

A special note: One of the great powers and advantages of defining your Personal Strategic Foundation is that books like the ones noted above now have much more value to you. That is, before defining your foundation, you may have read books like these with dozens of principles, ideas, and strategies, and experimented with them one by one. You may even have spent a lot of time trying to implement them effectively, with varying degrees of success. But now, with a clear foundation in place, you can assess the wealth of information in these collections and quickly determine IF they apply to your life; IF they are in alignment with who you are; and, IF they are, quickly and effectively apply their principles to your life in the way that works best for you.

In Closing...

Thank you for choosing our book and exploring the concepts and processes that make up *The Personal Growth Challenge™*. We believe that every one of us, in final analysis, has unique gifts and when discovered and used with intention, purpose and authenticity, they can, quite happily and productively, *Live from Strength*.

We are here for you throughout this process that is your life's journey. You can find additional resources, assessments, and information along with free downloads of all the exercises in our book at *www.LiveFromStrength.com*. You can also find access to other resources on our website including seminars, workshops, coaching services, informative articles, our monthly newsletter, and an open forum (blog) that will help you get the most out of the concepts, tools, and ideas discussed here in *Live from Strength*. Find us online. We'd love to hear from you!

May you have an abundantly successful and rewarding life. *Make it so!*

Warm regards,

Wayne Ottum

About the Author

Wayne H. Ottum is the President and founder of Ottum Enterprises, LLC, a firm dedicated to helping business owners, individuals and couples *Lead, Live and Love from Strength*™. Wayne is an expert at helping people act with confidence. Confidence that comes from discovering and aligning to one's **unique gifts** and developing a **clarity** of direction, purpose and values.

Wayne's entire educational and working career has been dedicated to human and business performance, improvement and growth. In 2003, Wayne founded Ottum Enterprises, LLC, and began partnering with business owners to help them create a clear direction, purpose and set of values, leading to the development of *"a business plan with real meaning;"* a plan that actually drives confident daily action for the entire company. This led to the development of the firm's flagship coaching process, *The Business Growth Challenge*™, which was the first in the company's *Lead from Strength*™ series.

Here is just one example of the impact of this process:

"Wayne Ottum provided me with guidance during the start up of my business. He understands strengths and communication styles and did an excellent job in guiding me to build a business completely in line with who I am. He is uniquely gifted at drawing one's best qualities to the surface to influence decisions in a positive way. My business is thriving because of all that Wayne brought to the conversation."
Marie M., Bellevue, WA

Through delivery of these services, Wayne quickly discovered the synergy of using these successful business principles to help individuals craft *"a business plan for life"* and created *The Personal Growth Challenge*™, the first service in the company's *Live from Strength*™ series and the processes detailed in this book. Here is another example from a satisfied client:

"The Personal Growth Challenge™ *provided me with a great experience that both challenged me to define what I wanted and taught me to recognize my unique talents and use them to improve my work and life experiences. As a result, I have been able to focus my actions and intentions on the correct path for me. Wayne's unique ability to see ahead and guide me, by challenging me to discover it within myself, made the outcome real and genuine and, therefore, a much stronger impact in my life."*
Misty F., Bellevue, WA

Wayne has now partnered with his wife Deborah Kiernan-Ottum to take these proven success principles and processes and applied them to relationships creating, *The Couples Growth Challenge*™, and the *Love from Strength*™

series of services. These coaching processes help couples clearly define the relationship they desire. They also learn to understand their own needs for intimacy, romance and passion, along with the needs of their partner, so that each of them can act confidently to create the relationship of their dreams.

To discover the power and fulfillment that comes when you "Love from Strength," check out Wayne and Deborah's book, *Create Intimacy... in as little as 8 seconds a day!* It is designed to show couples how easy it is to create, improve, and maintain the intimacy, romance, and passion in their life together! Here is what one of our readers said about the power of this book...

"I want to thank you for publishing a great book. My wife and I put it to valuable use this past week on our drive to Arkansas. We were in process of selling our properties so we could roam the country in new motor home. But on second thought, she felt our relationship not solid or fulfilling enough for that kind of life, so we opted to buy home in Arkansas to be near her 3 granddaughters. Having just read your book and attended your seminar, I realized I had not connected, not observed those 5 steps to intimacy. So I gave it a valiant effort to reform. During our 6 days in car together driving and sightseeing we took moments to read your book, answer the questions, fill out the charts, etc. And to be very candid about what we each wanted and perhaps lacked in the relationship.

It was part of an experience unlike any we had shared in nearly 10 years, including adventures around the world as friends. We discovered love for the first time on the trip and we give a lot of credit to the discussions stimulated by your common sense book. We're back dreaming together again.

Final Thoughts

Thanks bunches. I'll order 2 more books for each of my children so they can build their strong relationships even stronger."
Craig S, Lake Forest Park, Washington

Preview an excerpt from this powerful, ground-breaking book or purchase your copy today at our interactive website: *www.LoveFromStrength.com.*

Made in the USA
Charleston, SC
02 May 2014